ChangelingPress.com

Passionate Ink
Angela Knight's Guide to Writing Romance
Angela Knight

Passionate Ink
Angela Knight's Guide to Writing Romance
Angela Knight

ISBN: 978-1-60521-899-1

Publisher:
Changeling Press LLC
315 N. Centre St.
Martinsburg, WV 25404
ChangelingPress.com

Printed in the U.S.A.

Editor: Karen Williams
Cover Artist: Angela Knight

The individual stories in this anthology have been previously released in E-Book format.

Table of Contents

Passionate Ink
Angela Knight's Guide to Writing Romance
Angela Knight

The Forecast is in: the future of romance is hot and steamy. But riding the wave to success takes more than stringing together a couple of sex scenes or opening the bedroom door on your traditional romance.

In this newly updated edition of her classic "how-to," *New York Times* best-selling author Angela Knight shares the down and dirty details on writing erotic romances that will keep your readers haunting bookstores for your next book.

Knight discusses how to construct a story with wildly sexy heroes and determined, courageous heroines, the romantic conflicts that keeps them apart, and the external conflicts that drive them together. She explains how to write fight scenes as well as love scenes, and the surprising things they have in common. She also explores the construction of dynamic, absorbing plots in which love scenes are crucial to the romance and not just skippable porn breaks.

Write with Passionate Ink!

Introduction: The Joy of Writing Sex -- and Romance

It's considered an established fact that the American public doesn't read anymore, preferring movies and television. Yet romance publishing is a one point forty-four-billion-dollar industry. Somebody out there is definitely reading those books.

Trouble is, the original readership for romance -- those who devoured Barbara Cartland, Harlequins, and regencies -- is leaving the scene. Those who have taken their place like their romances darker -- outlaw heroes in motorcycle gangs or the Mafia. They're not shocked by the "F" word, and they see no reason anybody should skip a love scene's juicy details. They like sex, and unlike their predecessors, they weren't raised to believe "good girls don't." As a result, many longstanding publishing-industry assumptions about the romance readership no longer apply.

Thanks to self-publishing, and e-publishers like Changeling Press, readers have discovered the pleasures of no-holds-barred romance. Heroines don't have to worry about being "good girls" who only engage in carefully bland, vague sex. They can be just as passionate as heroes and enjoy edgier pleasures like bondage and submission -- or even dubious consent.

Twenty years ago, online readers weren't a very large share of the market, but now they're the majority. Traditional print publishers took note and realized the wave of the future might be hot and steamy.

Soon every print house started publishing erotic romance, and the market rewarded them as intrigued readers discovered the hotter, more sensual books.

I'm one of the authors who has reaped the

benefits. My erotic romances have appeared on the *USA Today*, *New York Times Publisher's Weekly*, and Barnes and Noble bestseller lists.

But that kind of success is more than a matter of stringing a few explicit sex scenes together. Just as in any other genre, best-selling erotic romance novelists write with the kind of creative power that seizes the imagination of fans. If you want to succeed as a writer, you need to do the same. Readers exploring an intriguing fad market will sample all kinds of things, but you want them coming back to *your* work.

Fads fade. Two decades ago, romances set during the Civil War and Indian wars were hot, but now those books would be very difficult to sell.

So why bother?

I believe that even when publishers are no longer interested in erotic romance, readers will still expect more than the pallid passion of earlier years. They'll still want steam, and it would be to your advantage to learn how to write it with as much power as you possibly can.

In this book, it's my objective to help you learn how to write the strongest novel you can. I intend to cover both basic and advanced concepts of romance writing, as well as techniques specific to erotic romance. I recommend you then follow up by reading some of the other books on writing that cover the specifics of plot and character construction in more detail. You'll find some of those books listed in the bibliography. The greater your knowledge of story construction, the higher your chances are of achieving publication -- and hopefully, best-sellerdom.

But what exactly is erotic romance?

Relevant Definitions

Though erotic romances aren't your mother's Harlequins, they're not porn either. The following are a few definitions to keep in mind.

Pornography: created with the sole purpose of creating sexual arousal in the reader as an aid to masturbation. The main character is usually a male with multiple partners. The story does not end in a monogamous relationship. Complicated plots, well-drawn characterization, and beautiful writing are rare, since readers are involved with the story for only a few minutes at a time.

Erotica: sexually explicit fiction with a more literary bent. A male hero is typical. Plot and characterization are better developed than in porn, and the writing style is literate. However, stable romantic relationships are usually not formed between characters; there are rarely the "happy endings" you'd see in the romance genre.

Women's Erotica: more akin to literary erotica than to romance. The main character is a woman who is a strong, well-developed character. She's on a voyage of self-discovery that may include experimentation with sexual practices such as bondage and submission, and she will often have more than one partner. These books may not end with the formation of a monogamous couple, though some of them do.

Mainstream romance: the focus is on the formation of a monogamous romantic relationship between a heterosexual or same-sex couple. Characterization is key, as is plot and romantic conflict. Sex may or may not be portrayed on the page, but if it is, it's given less focus than other plot elements. The language may be euphemistic, avoiding four-letter words, especially for genitals. There are rarely more than three love scenes in a novel, and they're often quite short, usually only a few pages at most. The protagonists form a monogamous couple by the end of the story. This kind of ending, called a Happily Ever After (HEA), is not only expected but demanded by editors and romance readers.

Erotic Romance: as in conventional romance, the focus of the story is on the formation of a romantic relationship between well-developed characters, but the love scenes receive more attention. There are more of them, and they are more detailed. Sex also plays an important role in driving the plot, which must be structured to allow for earlier and more frequent love scenes. The language tends to be blunter, with fewer euphemisms. As in traditional romance, an HEA is critical.

However, where mainstream romances end with a couple in a committed relationship, erotic romance may include several partners, same-sex or hetero. (Note that the more characters in the relationship, the harder it is to develop them into three dimensional characters. That's the reason I tend to limit my romances to four at most. Even then, it's tricky.)

Many readers are intrigued by the idea of alternative lifestyles, particularly those they'll never experience personally. Erotic romance gives them a safe way to conduct their explorations. Yet no matter how many people are in the relationship, readers want to know they'll stay together at the end. An erotic romance is still a *romance* -- first, last, and always.

Women, Pornography, and the Importance of Passion

Critics love to accuse erotic romance of being pornography, but anybody who's ever read porn knows there's a big difference.

Men read porn as a masturbation aid, but it takes them only about half the time it does us to reach a climax. You're not going to get into a whole lot of plot and characterization in fifteen minutes, so there doesn't tend to be much of either in most male porn. That's how you get female characters seducing the pizza delivery man.

Another factor is that male sexual arousal tends to be a bit simpler than ours, being based around sight and sensation more than anything else. We need more emotional involvement to become aroused, and it takes us much longer to come to a good roiling boil.

Why is there such a difference? I think women are hardwired for romance. Even when women have casual sex, somewhere in the back of their minds, they're still wondering if this guy is *the* guy.

Scientists think we evolved to look for love, not because of some girly hearts-and-flowers ideal, but out of cold-eyed practical necessity. Our primitive foremothers discovered the task of raising children alone in the wild was virtually impossible. Children require too much care to allow you to go off in pursuit of high-protein game. Basically, those mothers needed some guy to go out and bash the woolly mammoth over the head and drag it home for the kiddies.

Love and romance evolved, science tells us, to ensure bigger, stronger males hung around to assist in child rearing. True, the guy who spread his genetic material to as many women as possible stood some chance of siring kids that survived. But if he found one partner and stuck with her, that improved his offspring's chances even more.

So romance serves an evolutionary purpose, and that makes it incredibly powerful. That's why women look for romance even when they're reading for arousal.

I certainly do. When I read male-oriented porn back in college -- nobody was writing the female version in the early eighties -- I often found it hot, but ultimately unsatisfying. The female characters had all the personality and agency of blow-up dolls, while the heroes were self-absorbed and abusive. I wanted something more.

Some years ago, I conducted an informal survey of my readers and found they'd found male porn as unsatisfying as I had.

"The stories had no plot," one wrote in response to my questionnaire. "It was just sex. For me, if there is sex in a book, it's better when you know what brought the people together and what's going on with them."

Another agreed. "While it got me aroused, it also left me flat, ya know? Nothing to the story except getting off."

At the same time, though, many of the readers weren't completely satisfied with conventional romance either, at least not when it came to love scenes.

"I *hate* when a romance novel is full of life and color and sensual descriptions of fine food and great wine and starry nights on tropical islands -- and then the hero and heroine go to bed and suddenly I'm meant to cope with the most unintelligible euphemisms and strange descriptions of sex as some kind of mystical voyage to another dimension, hot waves lapping on distant shores, stars exploding in the abyss between two overlapping souls... Please! I read a category romance once where I had no idea that penetration had not occurred until it was mentioned in dialogue chapters and chapters on. I just assumed from all the fountains and waves and ripples of ecstasy that it must have done! It's just so phony, when otherwise competent authors do that."

"In most real relationships sex is a factor. Let's face it, no matter what we say or hope, we feel attraction to another before we ever feel love. Attraction, unfortunately, is often physical, which is desire/lust. Nothing wrong with that. It's a perfectly normal human reaction."

"In real life sexuality and sex are a big thing in relationships (or in most of them), and romances that eliminate that factor just seem stagnant. Erotic writers seem to understand the hungers/needs of readers. They don't shy away from it."

Another reader explained why she found erotic romance so powerful. "I had forgotten the edge, the raw emotion that first-time lovers feel for and with each other. Then I was introduced to erotic romance. This type of literature shows need and want, longing and desire without the flowered words that make me feel uncomfortable."

But though sex was important to the readers who answered the survey, they still wanted the same strong storytelling found in mainstream romance.

"Characterization and plot are very important; without it the sex is just bad porn. Erotic compared to romantic means the characters let nature take its course and sex was involved. Which is more realistic. So some sex is important, very important, but it's not THE most important thing."

"Sex and sexual tension are integral parts of erotic romance. It has to forward the plot, always. A character has to be believable. The people involved in an erotic romance are no different in motivation, thought processes, or needs than the characters involved in 'real life,' as long as the writer does it correctly."

What can we conclude from reading these comments? Erotic romance readers like vivid sexual storytelling, yes, but they also want believable, well-developed characters and strong plots. They're not just reading these stories as stroke material. They want the whole story, not just the sex. They also see the love scenes as a natural part of the romance that deserves just as much attention as any other part of the story.

In the coming chapters, I will examine how to structure a strong erotic romance in terms of plot, characterization, and dialogue. Other lessons will include the hero, the heroine, and the villain, as well as the nuts and bolts of writing a love scene. I'll dissect several of my own erotic scenes, and I'll explain why I structured them the way I did.

I'll also include extensive quotes from my readers on what they do and don't like, and why.

A Word of Caution

Some of the guidelines I give in this book are opinion, based on my experiences with readers and their reactions. Others are based on my tastes as a writer -- the kind of things I like to write.

For example, I write erotic romance as galloping adventures with lots of humor rather than dark psychological drama. But that's because dark psychological drama isn't my jam. If you like grimdark, write that. You should always write what you love.

Sometimes I'll give advice based on market wisdom. However, remember that the market shifts. Years ago, you couldn't sell a paranormal novel if your life depended on it, but now furred and fanged heroes are all over Amazon's best seller lists.

You may be the lucky soul who writes an "unmarketable" novel that takes off. Somebody will write the book that turns the market in a new direction, and it's always better to lead trends than follow them.

Don't forget that readers can be seduced into trying all kinds of things by the right author. Books with sports heroes were considered poison until Susan Elizabeth Phillips wrote a blockbuster series around her fictional Chicago Stars team. Now sports heroes get plenty of love, just like the rock stars who used to be verboten.

In short, if you find my advice doesn't ring true to you, follow your own instincts.

Be warned, though: a few of my guidelines are so hard and fast, you don't have a lot of wiggle room. Some situations and plots can alienate readers and damage your career. If I give you such a guideline, I'll explain why it shouldn't be flaunted.

Now let's start with the basics: planning your romance.

Section One -- Planning and Plotting
You won't arrive at your destination if you don't know where you're going

Chapter One: The Muse Speaks

Brainstorming and Researching Ideas

People love to ask writers where they get their ideas. The answer is usually "everywhere." Ideas can be sparked by books, television, movies, and news, not to mention the people and events in the writer's life.

What most non-writers don't understand is that there's more to a book than an idea. Give a dozen writers the same idea, and each of them will write a radically different book. That's because they'll use their own experiences, voice, outlook, and obsessions in realizing the concept.

This explains why professional writers don't get too upset about somebody else writing a book with the same core concept as the one they're doing. The two books are not going to be the same. (Though if you find chunks of unattributed identical wording, that's a sure sign of plagiarism -- and an impending lawsuit.)

Which doesn't mean all ideas are created equal.

Look for the Fun

When I'm brainstorming a novel, the first thing I think about is, "What would be fun to do?" I'm going to be living in this book for months, so it needs to be something I enjoy.

If you find a book torturous to write, readers will find it torturous to read. They'll sense your boredom and dislike and end up throwing the book across the room. Then they won't buy anything of yours again because you wasted their money.

I don't care what's hot right now, write only what you love. That goes triple for erotic romance. If you're one of those people who blushes bright pink at the thought of sex, you won't be able to write erotic stuff. No matter how skilled you are as a writer, the reader will sense your discomfort, and it will knock her right out of the scene.

Now, if you really want to write erotic fiction even though it pushes your comfort zone, that's something else. Start out with a few love scenes strictly for your own entertainment and see if you can't work through your reticence.

What do you do if you simply can't write whatever's hot right now? Write what does reach you on a deep emotional level, hot or not. I say that from personal experience.

Back in 2000, cowboys were big. I was desperate to find a New York publisher, but I had no interest whatsoever in writing a western. Instead, I wanted to write vampire romances, though at the time, the paranormal market was considered dead. As a compromise, I wrote a contemporary vampire novel with a hero who was a former Texas Ranger and Civil War veteran. He appeared in the heroine's dreams as a mysterious figure she called Cowboy, and the book featured flashbacks set in the Old West.

I liked the idea that nobody had done a romance with a cowboy vampire. At the time, vampires were always Victorian guys in opera capes. So Cowboy was a true departure, and I had an absolute ball writing his book.

Any time you can do something different from the standard clichés, go for it. The new approach will make the idea fresh and interesting for you, your editor, and your readers. Look at how Netflix's *Bridgerton* captured the public's imagination by casting people of color in an alternate universe version of Regency Britain. Same thing.

Trouble was, once I finished, I had to sell the

book. I sent my proposal to ten agents and got back ten rejection letters. Nobody was interested in what they considered an unmarketable paranormal romance.

Now, for the past several years, I'd been writing novellas for Red Sage's *Secrets* anthology series. Red Sage was the very first of the erotic romance small presses; it started publishing in 1995, years before the market took off.

I mentioned my unmarketable book to the Red Sage publisher, Alexandria Kendall, who had become a good friend. Alex told me she was thinking of trying a single title and would be interested in seeing mine. I sent it to her, and she bought it.

Between extensive rewrites and one thing or another, it was July, 2004 before *The Forever Kiss* was finally published, the month after my first Berkley book, *Jane's Warlord*.

I will never forget stopping by the mailbox that December and seeing the check from Red Sage. I opened it, telling myself not to expect too much as I pulled the check out. For a long time, I sat and stared at it in stunned disbelief.

There were a whole lot of zeroes on that check.

Readers had snapped up the "unmarketable" *Forever Kiss* like starving guppies in a fishbowl.

I was flat broke when that check arrived. I had quit my job to write full time, and I was trying to eke out an existence as a freelance writer for a weekly newspaper, a job that brought in about a hundred dollars in a *good* week. You can imagine what that check meant to me.

The next book of mine hit the *USA Today* list. It, too, was a vampire novel.

I succeeded because I had *not* followed the market. By 2004, westerns were on the way out.

Instead, I had written what I loved: a vampire hero in an erotic romance. Though I had no idea what I was doing at the time, I had combined what was about to become the two hot genres: paranormal and erotic romance. It was sheer dumb luck, but who cares?

The point is, I wrote what I loved, which is why I advise you to do the same. If you love writing erotic romance, write it. If you love writing westerns, write those. But whatever you write, look for a way to make it fresh and different.

I've heard it suggested that if you want to find the next hot thing in romance, look at what's popular on television and in film. In a couple of years, the reasoning goes, the same thing will heat up in publishing. I'm not sure if that's true, but it's worth a try.

In any case, when I'm trying to brainstorm a book, I go to a lot of movies, watch a lot of television, and read a lot of books. I adore big, splashy adventure movies in particular -- the kind brimming with special effects. Even when they don't give me ideas in themselves, all that action and color stimulates my subconscious. Soon ideas start bubbling to the surface.

Try it.

Romancing the Muse

When writing erotic romance, look for an idea in which sex is a major driver in the plot. Do not, however, plan a book that is nothing but a string of love scenes, because that's not going to sustain a novel. Think of sex as the icing on your erotic romance cake. You wouldn't eat a cake that's solid icing -- it would be cloying, maybe even a bit nauseating. You want your cake to have layers of conflict and drama, with moments of lush, creamy eroticism in between. That's what readers are looking for.

More on that later.

Sit down with a yellow pad and list things you'd like to write about. See if you can combine those elements in a different way.

When Cindy Hwang at Berkley asked me to write an erotic romance series for her, I spent the weekend trying to decide what I really wanted to do. I knew she wanted vampires, but I didn't want to do undead guys in opera capes.

So I started thinking about those things I really enjoy. Sword fights. Arthurian legend. Spies. Heroes who kick terrorist butt.

What if Merlin made Arthur and the knights of the Round Table immortal vampires? What if they feed on sex as well as blood? What if he gave them their abilities so they could defend humanity from its own self-destructive impulses? What if the Round Table had been working behind the scenes for centuries, fighting the forces of hate and chaos? What if they were fighting terrorists today?

Now, *there* was an idea I could run with.

And I did. Not only was it wildly successful, my Mageverse series was just as much fun to write as I expected.

So think about all the things you love best and see if you can combine them in new and interesting ways.

Research And Development

Once you have an idea you're interested in pursuing, start your research. Read two or three good, general books on the subject, and watch YouTube videos about it. (I read books on Arthurian legend, for example.) Often this research will give you additional plot ideas you can use to develop your story even more.

However, don't get so hung up on research that you never start your book. Research can easily become procrastination. If you need to know a specific detail once you start writing, hit the Internet and look it up. But remember, anybody can put anything on a website, including people who have no clue what they're talking about. Check multiple sources to make sure you have your facts straight.

That's crucial, because nothing yanks a reader out of a story faster than some detail she knows is wrong. Once she catches you in a mistake, you've lost her. Years ago, I read a futuristic romance in which the author repeatedly referred to the Milky Way galaxy as the Solar System. She hadn't even bothered to do the most basic research or fact checking. Between that and the fact that her hero wore silver lamé… Well, her book hit the wall with a meaty *thunk*.

Remember that your personal experience can be a source of inspiration and research, too. I was a newspaper reporter for ten years, which gave me a good understanding of law enforcement, firefighters, courts, and local government. As part of my job, I carried around a police scanner, which taught me the way cops talk when they're working. If you're going to write law enforcement characters today, YouTube is invaluable. Cops and police departments post training videos on everything from what the inside of a patrol car looks like to how to collect DNA evidence.

My werewolf books in the Mageverse series grew out of newspaper stories I did on two small town K-9 police officers and their dogs. I thought, "Hey, what if the dog was a werewolf?" And I was off and running.

When I decided to write my second werewolf

book, I went back to Woodruff K-9 Officer Doug Jones for a more detailed interview.

If you can find a source like Officer Jones, be careful to ask about the details, not just the big things. How does whatever he works with feel, taste or smell? For example, Jones told me crack has a strong odor of ammonia, like urine. He also described the routine of the job: the paperwork, what he does with evidence, how often he goes to court, what his work schedule is like. Using those elements added realism to the story -- which, considering it revolved around a werewolf, really helped its believability. Generally, the weirder a story is, the more it needs to be grounded in everyday details.

After *Master of Wolves* was published, I got wonderful emails from two female police officers complimenting me on the way I portrayed their jobs. And Officer Jones was thrilled.

I suggest that if you're going to do a book about a character with a given kind of job, whether it's a cop, firefighter, or hairdresser, find somebody that does that job and talk to them. Most people are more than happy to tell you anything you want to know, especially if you dedicate the book to them.

However, if you're dealing with a police department, you may have to go through channels first. Call and ask to talk to the public affairs or public information officer to learn how to arrange an interview. See if you can do a ride-along with an officer to get a feel for the job. Many departments allow that.

I also favor getting hands-on experience in what your characters do. My husband is a veteran cop, so I had him take me to the firing range so I could experience what it's like to shoot a gun. The pungent smell of nitroglycerin, the pale blue smoke, the buck of the pistol in my hands, that ear-shattering bang, all became details I call on whenever I write a gun battle.

I also took fencing, then used the things I learned in writing fight scenes. I discovered that when you're competing with someone and know you could get hit, you develop a kind of hyper-intense focus you wouldn't expect from reading books. I'd be willing to bet that effect is even more acute if your opponent's sword has an actual point. That experience has been invaluable when I write fight scenes.

Even historical pieces are open to hands-on research. See if you can find a group nearby that does historical re-enactments. I live near the Cowpens Revolutionary War National Park, and I love to go watch period reenactors fire their muskets and pitch their camps, all while wearing costumes that are historically accurate in every detail. That's a great place to pick up sensory stuff you can use. (One man told me his damp leather hunting jacket was like wearing five pounds of wet bacon.)

Look at the way they prepare food over a campfire. Sit down and talk to them about how life was lived in that time. People who do these sorts of re-enactments are fanatical about knowing every detail of the period, so they're great sources of information. Record the interview -- assuming they don't mind -- and snap tons of pictures. Save all thar stuff on your phone so you can refer to it later.

There's an old saying, "Write what you know" -- but that doesn't mean you can't learn more to write about.

I also suggest joining *Passionate Ink*, an online erotic romance writing group I helped found years ago. Passionateink.org offers all kinds of online classes on erotic romance techniques. This book started out as one of those classes, though I expanded it greatly for publication.

It's very difficult to be objective about your own book. You're too close to it, and you know what you intend by every sentence. A critique partner can read the manuscript with a fresh eye and see if it does what you want it to do.

I've had many critique partners over the years, and I've found them invaluable. There are times when I just can't come up with a solution to a particular plotting problem, even after days of banging my head against the wall. I often resolve the problem by talking to my CP, who frequently points out a solution that's been staring me in the face. And I've done the same for them, too.

All this planning, researching, and networking probably sounds like a lot of work. Well, it *is* a lot of work, but I think you'll find it pays off. There's no sweeter feeling than seeing your book sitting on a bookstore shelf.

Now, as to how to get it there…

Chapter Two: Plotting the Erotic Romance

The Story Question

As I mentioned earlier, erotic romance is structured differently from more conventional romances. To understand how, we need to start with a look at the engine that drives all fiction: the Story Question.

The Story Question is the one that keeps the reader reading. In a mystery, it's "Who killed the victim, and how will the detective catch him?" In a horror novel, it's "Will the protagonist survive?" In romance, the story question is, "Will the couple overcome the forces arrayed against them to reach their Happily Ever After?"

Note that the Story Question is rarely stated overtly. It's created in the reader's mind by the external and internal forces at work in the plot. How will these conflicts be resolved?

And there must be conflicts, or you don't have a story. If someone tells you your book is slow or even boring, it's because the conflicts aren't strong enough. You need conflicts with high stakes to get a reader invested in your book.

Every time you resolve a conflict, replace it with one even more serious. Our protagonists overcome their initial mutual distrust to become lovers. But just when we think an HEA is assured, we learn they've attracted the attention of a serial killer. Their situation worsens, intensifying the tension.

In conventional romance, there's often a secondary story question used to capture the reader's interest: "When will the couple finally make love?" Because sex is a primal human drive, that tremendous power as a story engine. This is especially true with a skilled author who can make readers share the characters' desire.

In any good romance, the writer begins building the sexual attraction between the protagonists from the moment they meet. At the same time, the author carefully establishes reasons why going to bed is a bad idea. Maybe their families are hereditary enemies. Maybe she's his boss, and she's worried about sexually harassing him. Maybe they're cops, and they're afraid they'll lose their jobs if they're caught fraternizing.

In fiction writing, such problems are called "external conflicts," because they're external to the characters.

Then the writer adds *emotional* reasons that keep them apart -- the "internal conflicts," so called because they act *within* the character. The heroine doesn't trust men because she was betrayed in the past. The hero is dealing with demons that make him fear falling in love and the vulnerability it entails.

At the same time, the author throws the couple together in a situation they can't escape while cranking up the attraction until they're dying to go to bed. The tension builds as readers wonder *when will they do it*?

What drives that kind of romance isn't sex, but *not* having sex. The minute the hero and heroine make love, that tension drains off. The writer must have a strong external or romantic conflict ready to replace it.

A non-romance genre version of this was *The X-Files*, in which FBI agents Dana Scully and Fox Mulder maintained a simmering sexual tension without ever exchanging more than a kiss. The show's creator, Chris Carter, was convinced the minute they Did the Deed, viewers would stop watching. He had good reason to think this, since programs like *Cheers* and *Moonlighting* lost much of their power and tension the minute their primary romances were consummated.

Now, the problem with building sexual tension that high and never paying off, as Carter did with *X-Files*, is that it becomes unrealistic and frustrating. To me, the most unbelievable aspect of that show wasn't the alien abductions, but that Mulder hadn't banged Scully's brains out by Season Three. The tension between those two was so high, in real life they'd have given in to it.

Too, Carter never really established *why* they didn't just sleep together when they were obviously in love. He didn't motivate their abstinence.

Which brings up another pitfall of teasing a sexual relationship that long: at some point, you've got to pay off. Mulder and Scully eventually had a baby, but it wasn't even conceived by sexual means. I feel more than a little cheated that we never got that promised romantic payoff in their relationship.

I've also encountered a romance version of this. The writer did a fantastic job of building the sexual tension between her couple. The hero was a dark and dangerous Alpha Male, and the scene where the two met was wildly sexy.

Trouble is, they didn't go to bed for a long, long time. Instead, they teased, and teased, and there was much angst over why they shouldn't have sex.

By Chapter Seven I was getting impatient, because their reasons for *not* doing it just weren't strong enough. For once, it was the hero keeping them out of bed: he thought he wasn't good enough for the heroine. Which, coming from such a rampant Alpha Male, sounded flatly unbelievable. Alpha Males *always* think they're good enough unless they're profoundly screwed up. In this case, that motivation wasn't present. And what does being "good enough" have to do with having sex, anyway? It sounded more like the kind of thing a woman would worry about.

The couple finally went to bed in the last quarter of the book -- for three lousy pages. Then the hero started agonizing again about how they couldn't be together for the exact same reasons he'd been using all through the previous fifteen chapters.

I literally slung the book against the wall. I almost never quit reading a book that close to the end, but I was so furious and frustrated with the writer, I didn't care what happened to those characters anymore.

If you build your book's tension based on a promised act, whether it's a love scene or the climactic battle with the villain, *you must pay off*. Otherwise, you'll end up with a frustrating anticlimax. The writer of that book should have made sure that love scene was the most steaming, fantastic sex imaginable because she'd teased it for 300 pages of a 400-page book. And it should have been a long, long scene, not a piddling three pages of mechanical coitus.

I suspect the problem was that the author didn't like writing sex, wasn't comfortable with it, and wanted to get it over with in as few pages as she could manage.

Now, if that's you -- and I assume it's not, or you wouldn't be reading this book -- don't tease the sex. Find some other engine for your story. Because I saw another book by that writer the other day, and I didn't buy it. Not because I *have* to have a sex scene, but because she had teased me mercilessly without delivering.

Finding The Engine For Your Erotic Romance
It should be obvious by now that this kind of

sexual tension is not going to work as the driving force in an erotic romance. Sexual tension of that type only works if the characters *don't* go to bed, and our characters hit the sheets early and often.

Now, I'm not saying there is no sexual tension between the hero and heroine in an erotic romance. But their getting into bed is not what keeps the reader flipping pages.

We need a different story question.

For erotic romance, the general story question is, "Will the couple overcome their conflicts and find their Happy Ever After?" The tension that drives most erotic romance is romantic tension rather than sexual tension. (Yes, I know all romances are driven by that question to some extent, but in many mainstream romances, the heavy lifting is done by sexual tension.)

Thus, when you start structuring your erotic romance, you must decide what forces are going to stand in the way of your protagonists becoming a permanent couple. These barriers must be so strong, the reader is driven to discover how you overcome them.

Remember the prequel *Star Wars* trilogy? Regardless of what you may think of *The Phantom Menace, Attack of the Clones* and *Revenge of the Sith*, they were driven by a wonderful story question: "How does Anakin Skywalker evolve from heroic Jedi Knight to murderous Darth Vader?" We knew he was going to end up as Darth; we knew Obi Wan would cripple and scar him, but he was so heroic and the two men were such close friends, we had trouble imagining how this was going to happen.

But we really wanted to find out.

You must set up a story question every bit that strong to drive your novel. And it's going to be tough, because erotic romance demands that your hero and heroine spend a lot of time making love. This means they can't start out hating each other, as couples sometimes do in romances, because it wouldn't be believable that they'd hop into bed that fast with somebody they disliked.

So create a set of circumstances that drive them together and keep them there, while simultaneously making a long-term relationship seem virtually impossible.

In my paranormal erotic romance *Master of the Moon*, heroine Diana London is in her Burning Moon -- the werewolf equivalent of heat. She needs to have sex desperately, but an ordinary human partner is out of the question, because she might inadvertently turn him into a werewolf.

Her prayers are answered by a handsome Sidhe male -- a fairy -- from an alternate magical universe. He isn't human, so she doesn't have to worry about him becoming a werewolf. Her werewolf pheromones attract him, so he's just as hot for her as she is for him.

Now, if that was all there was to the conflict, the reader wouldn't be all that worried about whether they'd end up together. In fact, they might lose interest and go read something else.

But my hero isn't just any Sidhe -- he's Llyr Galatyn, King of the Sidhe. The King of the Fairies isn't going to marry some mortal werewolf. His people won't accept her. *And* Llyr's brother Ansgar has been trying to seize his throne by methodically murdering every one of Llyr's wives and children. If Diana gets too close, she'll become a target too. *And* Ansgar is trying to kill Llyr. *And* Diana is the city manager of a small town with a highly moralistic population which does not approve of her fooling around with this weird guy. *And* a vampire serial killer is in town, and Diana and Llyr have to capture her before she kills anyone else. *And* Ansgar hires the vampire to kill Llyr...

You see how this works. As the book goes on, I added more and more reasons to keep them apart. Every time I took care of one problem, I introduced another.

The idea is to keep the reader curious. Yes, this couple is having fantastic, toe-curling sex, and they're obviously falling in love. But there are so many forces working to keep them apart, it isn't at all clear how my hero and heroine are going to overcome them. The fact that they will win is a given -- just like Anakin becoming Darth -- but the reader wants to know how.

So when you're working on the plot of your book, the first thing you need to determine is your specific story question -- the conflict that will keep the reader flipping pages to find out how you resolve it.

The question is, how do you pull that off?

Man Against Woman

All fiction is about conflict.

If you're planning a book where your protagonists go to bed and have lots of great sex for 400 pages without so much as an argument, it's not going to work. Your readers may enjoy that first meeting and the first sex scene or two, but after that, they're going to start looking for some kind of plot.

In that survey I did, readers were very definite on the importance of plot and conflict.

"I don't read erotic romance to get a quick rush or shut off my brain," one of them wrote. "Everything I read had better challenge me mentally and emotionally, or it's not worth reading. I love a plot that forces at least two people to change their perceptions of themselves, the world around them and each other, for better or worse. There have to be moments in which the characters see the darker part of themselves and make a choice. I love action. I know there are snickers on that one, but I love action outside the bedroom too. Give me something besides a bedroom and a couple of strangers, PLEASE. I need something to happen, changes, lives, wars, give me stimulus or I can't read it."

She wasn't the only one. "Hot sex scenes aren't enough to sell me a book if there's not something to hang it all together."

"If there is no plot, no characterization or setting, the chances of me actually paying for the book is slim to none. I am not interested in just one big orgy for no apparent reason that lasts 200 plus pages."

Yet that doesn't mean they just want action plots without strong romances either.

"Sometimes I want action and adventure... sometimes I want thrills and chills... sometimes I want violence and gore... but without a hero and a heroine to see each other through the bad stuff, have great sex and find love with each other, it's just empty words on a page."

The foundation of creating the kind of story they're talking about is crafting a good conflict between strong characters.

But what is conflict? You may remember the three kinds of fictional conflict from your high school English classes: Man against Man, Man against Nature, and Man against Himself. All three of those may appear in romances, but the kind I'm going to discuss here is Man Against Man -- or Woman.

This kind of conflict is born when people with opposing goals start butting heads over what they want.

Debra Dixon has written a wonderful book on this called *Goal, Motivation, and Conflict* that has become the must-read guide for romance novelists. Go to any romance writers' conference, and somebody will mention *GMC* at least once. I strongly recommend you buy it if you're serious about becoming a published romance novelist.

The essential idea behind the book is to help authors work out the internal and external goals, motivations, and conflicts of their characters, and how those conflicts intensify one another. Before I start a book, I always write GMC charts for every one of my major characters, including the villains. I then use the charts to plot my book.

Here are the GMC charts I used to create my first novel, *Jane's Warlord*. You'll see that each character has an internal and external goal, a motivation for those goals, and a set of conflicts they must overcome to reach them.

The internal GMC refers to the character's psychological conflict. It's important to have a set of internal GMCs, or your character is going to end up cardboard. A character's actions must be driven by their internal goals and neuroses, not the plot's demands, or they won't seem like real people.

The external goal, motivation, and conflict is born of the external situation the character faces: catching the bad guy, saving the farm, winning the protagonist's love.

Plotting Guide: Jane's Warlord
Hero: Baran

Goal:

Internal: To be in control; he despises being vulnerable

External: To kill the alien serial killer who has targeted Jane and return to his own time.

Motivation

Internal: Baran survived sexual torture at the hands of a Xer warrior, but the rest of his team was killed. This left him with a huge burden of guilt that he failed those who depended on him. He was bred to be a protector, and he has a warrior's powerful sex drive and the strength to go with it. As a result, he hungers for women, but he's afraid of hurting them with his superhuman strength. Particularly Jane, whom he considers even more delicate and vulnerable than the women of his own time.

External: The Vardonese are at war, and he's needed back home to captain his ship. But he won't be allowed to return home until Druas is caught.For him, his captaincy is the ultimate in control. He takes orders from Vardonese high command, but in space, he's the only authority. It's the job he always dreamed of, and he worked hard to get it.

Conflict

Internal: He begins to fall for Jane, and he certainly hungers for her sexually, but he considers her too fragile. Then when she begins to really deal with the situation and take control, he feels uneasy. He realizes she's not like the women of his own time, and he has no idea how to deal with her.

External: The alien Druas is just as inhumanly powerful as he is, and has been traveling the time stream killing at will.

Heroine: Jane Colby

Goal

Internal: To prove her independence, intelligence and capabilities to herself and everyone else. To overcome her fear of Druas.

External: To keep Druas from killing her or anybody else. When she fails to keep the other women safe, it eats at her.She also wants to get rid of Baran and the serial killer and get back to her nice, normal life.

Motivation

Internal: Jane's father has always made her feel like a failure. She's struggled with a sense of being unworthy for years, so she works deadly hours in her drive to succeed. Baran's dismissal of her abilities makes her feel like the failure her father always painted her. She hungers for his respect just as she hungers for him sexually.

External: Colbys have run the Tayanita Times for a century; the paper is the heart and soul of the town. She was raised to believe that as a Colby and a journalist, she has a duty to the public. That includes fighting anything that would endanger the public welfare -- including serial killers.

Conflict

Internal: She finds Baran's belief that she must be protected maddening. He sees her as someone to have sex with and protect, but not as someone to love, and it drives her nuts. She finds him incredibly sexy and heroic; he's every woman's dream. But he's got a dark side, such as his need to dominate her. It bothers her that she finds that perversely arousing. But she's determined to teach him that just because she likes being tied up, that's not an indication she's his inferior.

External: Druas has changed his MO in that he's begun doing more than just killing with a razor. He's also setting fires and trying to cause as much destruction as he can. She knows the police can't deal with him; only Baran can. But Baran doesn't know the town or modern customs, and that gets both of them in trouble.

You need GMCs for antagonists too. It's important to get inside the heads of all the characters so none of them end up two-dimensional.

Jane's and Baran's GMCs are a good illustration of the way conflict works in an erotic romance. You'll notice that the goals for each character conflict directly with the goals for the other.

Baran's goal is to be in control; he despises being vulnerable. Jane's is to prove her intelligence and capabilities to herself and everybody else. It's easy to see how Jane's need to prove herself would cause her to butt heads with Baran. She doesn't want to sit back and be protected. She believes she has a responsibility to the people of Tayanita to help find this serial killer, and she intends to help Baran do this whether he likes it or not. After all, Baran doesn't know the town, the time, or the people, so he needs her help to find his way around and deal with the local bureaucracy.

But this interferes with Baran's need to be in control, and it drives him crazy.

Now, each of these characters needed a good reason to have the attitudes they do. You can't just hang "needs to be in control" around the neck of a character and be done with it. He must have a backstory that created his goals and hang-ups, or he's cardboard.

In Baran's case, he fell in love with a female Vardonese warrior when he was eighteen. Baran and his lover were sent to rescue a Vardonese scientist who had been kidnapped by invading aliens called the Xer.

But when they got to her, the scientist refused to leave without the research the Xer had taken from her. When Baran tried to recover the research, they were all captured.

He ended up tortured and raped, and both his lover and the scientist were murdered. Baran eventually escaped, but his entire team was killed trying to rescue them. He blames himself, because when the civilian insisted on having her way, he didn't stand up to her.

So Baran's attitude toward Jane is that she is damn well going to do what she's told, period. Jane, on the other hand, was raised by a controlling, abusive father she strongly suspects of murdering her mother. He spent years verbally abusing her until he finally died the year before the book starts. As a result, she doesn't deal well with dominant men. And the whole idea of being the target of a serial killer and ending up murdered like her mother is just too chilling for words.

Under normal circumstances, a pair of characters like Baran and Jane wouldn't stay in the same zip code for more than ten minutes. They wouldn't be able to stand each other. But I set up the plot so that they need each other desperately. Baran needs to save Jane from the serial killer so he'll be allowed to return to his own time. Jane does not have a prayer against the super-powered killer without Baran's help. They *must* work together.

But for them to fall in love and have a believable HEA, they must also resolve all these conflicts, or the reader won't believe they'll stay together. Throughout the course of the book, incidents force Baran and Jane to see each other in a new light. Jane discovers that though Baran can be dominant and overwhelming, he is also compassionate and heroic, two things her father was not.

Baran discovers that Jane is intelligent and capable, despite being only human. In the final conflict, Baran must trust Jane to serve as the bait for the villain without getting herself killed, while Jane must find the courage to confront the killer. In so doing, she puts her own fears to rest. This ending resolves both the external conflict and the characters' romantic and internal conflicts at the same time.

Pick up *Goal, Motivation, and Conflict* for a more detailed explanation on the grid and the way to use it in planning and resolving conflicts.

The only problem with GMC charts is that they don't specifically deal with the romance. They're great devices to work out big conflicts, but I decided I needed another grid that would help me refine and think through the elements of the romance plot.

I created the following simple grid with that in mind. Again, I'll use *Jane's Warlord* as the example.

Jane's Warlord: Romantic Conflict Chart

His initial impression of her:

> She's lush and lovely, but she is incapable of defending herself. He's going to have to make her obey his orders for her own good. She's nothing like the strong, capable warrior he'd loved and lost.

Her initial impression of him:

> He's ruthless and powerful, and is too much like her abusive father.

What changes that impression for him:

> He comes to respect her intelligence and courage as she helps him track Druas down.

What changes that impression for her:

> He shows compassion to her, and he agonizes over the women he fails to save.

What first attracts him to her:

> Her delicacy and femininity. Before they meet, he also discovers her nightgown, and becomes aroused by her scent.

What first attracts her to him:

> He's tall, muscular, and immensely powerful; the kind of man she secretly fantasizes about.

What he admires about her character:

> She refuses to yield to her fear, even knowing how much danger she's in. She's

even willing to go toe to toe with him, despite his obvious physical superiority.

What she admires about his character:

> His determination to protect the helpless from Druas, a time-traveling serial killer.

What most annoys him about her:

> She refuses to back down and do what she's told, even when she's obviously not capable of defending herself against Druas.

What most annoys her about him:

> His attempts to dominate her into doing what he wants.

How she completes him:

> She teaches him to let go of his guilt over his team's death.

How he completes her:

> He teaches her she does have the ability to meet her fears and defeat them.

Why he thinks it will never work:

> He's from the future, and he's going to have to go back. She's just a human, and he's a Warlord.

Why she thinks it will never work:

> He's from the future, and he's going to leave her. Even if she could go to the future, she could never survive there.

What he learns so that it does work:

> He's destined to take her to the future with him.

What she learns so that it does work:

> She can learn to adjust to life in Baran's world if it means being with him.

If you use both GMC and this Romantic Conflict chart, you should be able to work out the major issues in your romantic plot before you sit down to write. That can save you a great deal of time and headaches. If your conflicts aren't strong enough, your book may blast along for the first couple of chapters, only to wander off into a dead end as you run out of dramatic steam.

I've fallen prey to this myself in an earlier draft of a book that went on to become a bestseller, *Master of Wolves*. I adored the initial idea for the book. My hero, Jim London, is a werewolf who goes undercover as a police dog to catch the killer of his best friend. The heroine is his K-9 handler, Faith Weston, who has no idea he's a werewolf.

As I first envisioned it, the primary romantic conflict was that Jim fell in love with Faith in dog form long before she had any idea he was human. There's an obvious problem with that idea: if she thinks he's a dog, he can fall in love with her all he wants, but you still don't have a romance. You need at least two lovers to have a romance. Anything less is stalking.

There's a lesson there: when you come up with an idea you love, sit down and see whether it will actually work within a romance structure. In romances, you really must have the protagonists together and interacting within at least the first two chapters. And they can't be separated for longer than a chapter or so. Though I did that in *Master of Wolves* -- technically -- the fact that one character thought the other was a dog pushed the romance structure a little too much.

I had to gut and restructure the book twice to reveal the hero's secret earlier and construct a romantic conflict between them. Even so, the romantic conflict wasn't as strong as it was in *Jane*. Most of the book's tension came from the external conflict with my antagonists. I got it to work, but it took me months longer than it should have, and I had to ask for extensions on my deadline.

If I had spent time working out a really solid romantic conflict like the one I had for Jane and Baran, the book would have been much easier to write, and I wouldn't have had all those false starts. So do your homework!

Having said that, how do you put these charts to use?

Some people write by the seat of their pants. They have some idea where they're going, and they work their way through the book to the last page. Personally, I'm a plotter, and I get into deep trouble when I don't think things out in detail ahead of time.

If you're a newbie, I strongly suggest you start out doing full plots of your books. Unlike Nora Roberts or Susan Elizabeth Phillips, you probably don't understand the mechanics of a romance well enough to write by instinct. Working out a full plot will allow you to make sure all the ingredients are in place, so you can concentrate on writing without driving yourself crazy.

The AK Plotting Process

I used to take Post-It® notes, each with a major scene on it, and arrange them on a big cardboard backboard. But they kept falling off, and the backboard was huge and hard to work with.

Then I discovered a program called Scrivener, which is essentially the computer version of my backboard and Post-It® system. If you don't want to buy the program, you could also work with physical note cards or Post-its. Or, for that matter, a legal pad. Whatever works best for you.

What I do is block out the major scenes of the book, with one card per scene. I assume that for a 100,000-word book, I need twenty chapters of about 5,000 words each. I usually have two to three major scenes a chapter. That's fifty to sixty scenes.

The first scene card might read something like: "Jane talks to a detective at the scene of a murder where Druas has just killed his first victim." The next card could be, "Baran and his talking wolf partner, Freika, break into Jane's home, determined to establish themselves as her bodyguards. When she returns, they confront her."

Basically, what you're doing is blocking out the logic of the story. Think of the first thing a character would reasonably do: "Baran and Freika break in and confront Jane." Then you decide what the other character's reaction to that act would be. "Jane panics and attacks Baran, managing to blind him by throwing a bottle of perfume in his eyes. She runs, but Freika catches her before she can escape."

It's like a chess game, with every character making moves intended to achieve their goals. That's why the charts come in so handy; you use them to plan each character's reactions.

Plotting this way makes writing the dreaded synopsis much, much easier. Just write a paragraph describing your major characters and their internal and external conflicts. Then follow that with a line or two for each of your scene cards. And yes, you do include the ending in the synopsis, because the editor wants to be sure you know how to resolve your conflicts. You'll find one of my synopses in this book's appendix.

That said, don't be surprised if your plot evolves once you start writing. I always expect changes as the story hits the page. Characters and events crop up that I didn't expect, adding richness and complexity. But the rough plot framework I created keeps me going in the right direction.

Plotting The Erotic Romance

This technique can be used to plot virtually anything. If you're working on an erotic romance, however, you need to pay particular attention to the role of sex in the plot. Erotic romance works best when the act of making love plays an important role in the action. For example, I specify that Warlords have a powerful sex drive, so Baran is really interested in making love, especially when he's just been in battle. He also uses sex to try to dominate Jane, so it plays into the conflict between them.

In my Mageverse series, sex is just as important. Only men become vampires in the Mageverse, while women become Majae, or witches. Collectively, they're called the Magekind. In most vampire stories, a character becomes a vamp after being bitten by a vampire. But in the Mageverse, I decided the act of making love triggers a spell that transforms the character.

Unfortunately, some people can't handle the

transformation and go insane. They may even kill their lovers. This creates all kinds of built-in tension for everyone.

When you're thinking through your book, make sure sex plays a pivotal role in the plot. And as with my murderous-lover twist, look for ways to make your characters' lives as difficult as possible. Any time you can add some nasty little complication, you can make the book more exciting.

Logical Love Scenes

You need to be careful you don't just stick in a sex scene somewhere the characters should be doing something else. If the protagonists know there's a serial killer getting ready to murder a woman, that's obviously not the time to make love. The love scene should fall *after* they've saved the woman, or at some point in the story where they really can't do anything else.

Maybe the protagonists are snowbound in a blizzard, or they're vampires and they'll burst into flames if they try to step outside in the sunlight. Either way, it's got to make sense, or your reader will think your characters are idiots. That's not the impression you want.

You need characters the readers will admire and root for. But how do you create them?

Section Two -- Characterization
Heroes, Villains, and Others

Chapter Three: The Man of Her Dreams

Protagonists and Antagonists

Protagonists and antagonists often seem to assume certain natural roles in romances. Antagonists drive the external conflict, for example -- it's their actions that set the rest of the story in motion. The villain kills his first victim, steals some priceless object or sends a threatening letter to the heroine.

In a heterosexual romance, the heroine sets the sexual pace; the hero can push all he likes, but she's the one who decides when and if they make love. Otherwise, it's rape.

In a male/male romance, one of the men is often the smaller of the two. He becomes the female reader's surrogate and takes on the plot functions served by heroines in het romances.

But the sexual heat ultimately comes from the hero. That's not to say the heroine can't make the first move -- she certainly can. But it's the hero that really turns the readers -- and the heroine -- on.

Heterosexual women respond to men. You can have a female character who is hot as a pistol, whom male readers would fall violently in lust with, and she's not going to do a single thing for your het female readership if you pair her with a nebbish hero. On the other hand, you can have a heroine who isn't particularly sexy, but if a hot Alpha decides he wants her and is going to get her, you've got instant heat. That's part of the fantasy that undergirds female-centered romance.

The right hero is extremely important to a good erotic romance. In a plot with a strong action component, that's usually going to be an Alpha male. A best-friend "beta" type is fine for romantic comedy, but when the bullets start flying, women want some big, protective stud around to keep them alive. Assuming they themselves aren't the dangerous one in the relationship.

Having said that, other kinds of heroes can work well in erotic romance. I like Alphas, personally, but you can do any kind of guy you find sexy, as long as you can build a good conflict around him.

I focus on Alphas in this book because their personalities make for built-in conflict when you pair them with a strong heroine. Alphas are natural leaders -- that's pretty much the definition of an alpha -- with a strong protective streak and a fierce confidence in their own abilities. Give a man like that an independent, intelligent heroine disinclined to take orders, and you'll get instant sparks. He wants to protect her, while she thinks she can protect herself. What's more, she may believe she can protect *him*, which drives him straight up the wall. She may even be right if you want to really make him crazy.

The hero's protective attitude doesn't have to be sexist to strike sparks; it can simply be realistic. He's probably four or five inches taller and sixty or more pounds heavier, all of it muscle. He has the upper body strength to bench press his own weight, something she probably can't do. He may have more combat or investigative experience, depending on the storyline.

Yet she's his equal in intelligence, courage, and will. What's more, she may be right about an aspect of the situation he's misread. A set-up like that can cause all kinds of lovely conflict that results in his growing respect for her.

That's important, because as I've said, the more conflict you give a book, the easier it is to write. I've written stories in which *everyone* has opposing internal and external goals and motivations. Even the villain and his chief henchman were in conflict. With all those factors in play, the reader doesn't know what's going to happen next. That makes it easier to keep editors and readers alike intrigued.

Turning Up The Heat

When it comes to sexual conflict and sizzle, the hero is the driving force of the book. Generally, women readers are going to respond best to a physically imposing man, but there's more to an Alpha male than that.

One of the most remarkable Alphas I've ever read is Miles Vorkosigan, the hero of Lois McMaster Bujold's wonderful Vorkosigan science fiction series. Miles's mother was the victim of a chemical gas attack when she was pregnant with him, and he was born with extremely brittle bones. As a result, he's under five feet tall, painfully thin, and was even hunchbacked at one point. Yet Bujold makes Miles so wildly sexy and charismatic that you have no difficulty at all believing that gorgeous women fall madly in love with him. I recommend reading the Vor series just for a look at how to write a kick-ass Alpha male who is so much more than muscle.

First, Miles is brilliant -- half military genius, half charismatic con artist who seduces people into following him with a combination of humor, intelligence, and unflinching courage. People who meet Miles are at first contemptuous, then bemused. Before long, all that charisma starts getting to them, and he's got them doing exactly what he wants.

I'd love to write a protagonist like that. He'd be a blast to do.

Generally, though, it's easier to make your

readers hot for a hero who is physically handsome. That means you as a writer need to spend a certain amount of time on the way he looks. Of course, the drawback to this is what you find sexy in a man may not be what your readers find sexy. I like a buff guy while other women like a lanky marathon runner. So if you start giving me a description that reads "wiry," I'm going to think "skinny," which is *not* going to turn me on. It's better to use a word like "leanly muscular," which is vague enough to let me fill in the blanks with something I like.

Avoid using an actor in your description. First, he may do something to put a bad taste in everybody's mouth. Too, referring to actors in the hero's description dates the book. Robert Redford was gorgeous back in the day, but twenty-something readers have never seen Redford as anything but the leathery-looking guy who plays villains and runs that film festival. Again, not the association you want.

Looks aside, the real key to sexual attractiveness in a man is attitude, dialogue, and action.

Self-confidence is a big part of why we love Alpha males. Whether he's in the bedroom or tracking down a killer, he's the best there is at what he does, and he knows it. However, he's not going to stand around and brag. He's got more important things to do, and besides, he doesn't need to boast. You'll figure it out on your own.

But though he won't stoop to bragging, his confidence shines through in his dialogue. It's one of the things that makes him both attractive and infuriating to his romantic partner. Couple that with blazing sexuality, and you get an explosive combination.

Here's a scene from *Jane's Warlord*:

"You're really not a nice man."

Baran bent his head to study her nipples with predatory interest. "No." Slowly, he raked his teeth over one pink tip, sending pleasure bolting up her nerves. "But then, I don't think you want a nice man."

Gasping, she let her head fall back against the wall and closed her eyes. "Not right now, no."

Baran, my genetically engineered hero from the future, is both powerful and sexually skilled. He knows the heroine wants him, and he knows how to increase that desire. The taunting edge in his dialogue only makes her -- and the reader -- hotter. Dominance is a tricky characteristic, since it can also read as "asshole." But it can work well in turning up the heat. If, that is, you can pull it off without turning your Alpha into a jerk.

One way to avoid jerkdom is to give the hero a strong moral code. He may be stronger and faster than other people, but he believes those abilities carry certain responsibilities. He certainly doesn't use them to bully his partner.

"Dominant Alpha males are great," one reader wrote in response to my survey, "as long as they remember that respect and dignity are basic human needs. The 'taking care of the little woman because she couldn't survive without big ol' me' thing just ticks me off -- yet 'caring for you while you are vulnerable' is entirely different. To me the key is 'listening.' Does he listen and hear her concerns and worries, etc.? Or does he 'assume' he just knows because he has testicles?"

Basically, your hero must treat your heroine like an intellectual equal, if not a physical equal. Yes, he may be more powerful than she is, but he must respect her skills too. Or, if he doesn't in the beginning, he should by the end of the book.

"(I) dislike any male that thinks the woman is automatically too stupid to think for herself or unable to look out for herself," another reader wrote. "It's mildly acceptable at the start of a book if he's got some significant experience, but by the end he should be accepting that the woman has her own strengths even if she can't do things the way he would."

"Alpha males are great as long as I'm convinced that he loves her and wouldn't hurt her. As long as he pays attention to her and really wants to make her happy. With the emphasis on making her happy and not just making her smile so that his life is easier or so that he gets laid. Actually listening and paying attention is what'll make him attractive. If he tries, I'm willing to forgive a lot."

Now I'm going to give you a case of psychic whiplash by contradicting myself. You've probably spotted the problem yourself: how do you have a conflict with this guy? He respects women, he listens, and he's attentive. This is the kind of man that the heroine can chew out, and he'll apologize profusely and back down.

Do *not* try to write a hero so nice, he's gummy. True, a romance with a man like that would be comfortable and safe -- but it would also be about as exciting as watching grass grow.

I think this is one of the problems in mainstream romances. We're portraying men the way feminist ideals say they should be -- respectful and consensus-building.

Yet women like bad boys. There's something seductive about a guy in leather with a dangerous attitude and a smart mouth. Our instincts respond to the big, brawny stud who loves a good fight and a good fuck -- in more or less that order.

In fact, this may be one reason why Dark Romance is gaining popularity so fast -- writers feel free to write dominant heroes with more of an edge than they could get away with in more mainstream books.

So how do you strike that delicate balance between jerk and wildly sexy stud?

One of the best authors around at pulling off this hat trick is J.R. Ward. Ward's Black Dagger Brotherhood series deals with a gang of huge, deliciously handsome vampires who are about as far from "nice" as you can get. One is a blind king who hates humans, another is a scoundrel who runs through women like toilet paper, while a third is a scarred, menacing figure who despises anything female.

You have to admire the sheer chutzpah of a writer who'd make a sadomasochistic misogynist named Zsadist into a romance hero. Yet Ward hits the New York Times list every time one of her books comes out. Readers love those characters, and so do I.

How does she do it?

She carefully motivates each Brother's particular flaw. The blind vampire king was tortured by humans when he was a young man. In truth, he loathes himself far more than he does humans.

So naturally, it's a half-human woman who helps him rediscover himself and let go of his guilt in *Dark Lover*.

In *Lover Eternal*, Rhage is a womanizer because

he's been cursed to transform into a villain-eating dragon. Blowing off sexual steam with an endless series of women is the one way to control his curse.

In *Lover Awakened*, Zsadist was raped repeatedly by a female vampire for centuries until he grew to loathe women. In fact, he even hates his own penis. It takes a woman almost as badly wounded as he is to heal him. That book is driven by the absorbing story question of how on earth anyone that wounded and dangerous could ever have a happy ending. Amazingly, Ward pulls it off.

But there's a trick to it. She establishes her heroes and their particular hang-ups *before* she brings them together with the heroines. Then she has the hero realize almost immediately that the heroine is the woman for him. What's more, he's willing to kill anybody who so much as chips her nail polish. There's a lesson here: *any character is a lot more sympathetic when there's someone or something he loves.*

Then Ward gives each of her bad boy heroes a woman willing to stand up to him, and we get to watch the sparks fly. Slowly, her heroines break through the heroes' tough defenses. Love blooms -- and heals.

I did something similar in *Jane's Warlord*. Like Ward, I began by establishing my hero's extravagant sexuality.

In the opening chapter, Baran breaks into my heroine's house, planning to establish himself as her bodyguard whether she likes it or not. After telling his talking wolf sidekick not to eat her cat, he discovers her negligee on her bed and is struck by its delicate size:

> Baran wondered what her soft, pink mouth
> would taste like, how her breasts would fill

his hands, if her skin would feel as silken as it looked. His cock hardened, going long and tight behind his fly. With a soft growl of hunger, he rolled his head against the gown in his hand, drinking in her smell, the slide of the slippery fabric against his face, the rasp of lace. He imagined thrusting into her for the first time, feeling all that wet arousal gripping him, milking him...

It had been far too long since he'd had a woman in his sleep sack. Days, weeks -- he couldn't remember and didn't much care. All that interested him suddenly was this woman, this Jane Colby, with her pretty eyes and small, lush body.

He breathed in her scent again as his hunger spiraled, tightening in demanding coils around his balls. The same genetic engineering that enhanced his strength made his lust even more intense than a normal man's. Now that suddenly hot-burning need sent carnal images spinning through his mind -- Jane, naked, on her back, on her knees, spread and ready for him, plump sexual lips slick with thick female cream...

A rumble of need vibrating his chest, Baran opened his eyes and glared down at the bundle of red silk in his fist. He ached to open his fly and wrap the cool, slick fabric around his cock...

Better not. Jerking off in her negligee would send a worse message than eating the cat.

The intent of the scene is to establish Baran's potent reaction to the heroine. Readers find such intense desire in a man very erotic.

"I always love it when the hero is almost out of his mind with lust," one of them wrote. "When he knows immediately what, who, he wants. When I feel like I'm being given some real insight into the workings of the male mind. The scene involving Baran in Jane's bedroom before she gets home, for instance, is a fantastic set up, wonderful stuff. So is Emma Holly's introduction of Zach and his first impressions of Julia in *The Top of her Game*. Sometimes that glimpse into a man's mind, of what he wants to do, of his secret desires, is almost more erotic than what happens when he actually gets to play."

Note her comment about being given real insight into the male mind. That's important.

When we write, we play the characters in our heads like actors. If you try to play the hero as reacting the way *you* would react, you're going to get into trouble. That's because we as women are taught to handle problems very differently than a man would.

Recently, somebody sent around one of those joke emails purporting to show the way a guy really thinks. One of those "guy rules" said, "Don't tell us about a problem unless you want us to suggest a solution. That's what your girlfriends are for." Though it was a joke, I thought it was dead on.

Alpha protagonists don't like to make decisions by committee. Instead, he wants to decide what to do and just do it. This approach can be a serious source of conflict with the heroine, who, being female, wants to discuss the problem and build a consensus.

Then there's the emotional angle. Your Alpha's feelings are every bit as strong as his heroine's, but his brain isn't wired the same way. Scientists tell us the brain has two hemispheres, one of which experiences emotion, while the other uses language. In women, the two are well-connected, which is why we love to talk about our feelings. Yet for some reason, the connections are much less established in men.

So like most men, your hero is going to find it difficult to put his emotions into words. He'd rather communicate with action -- sex, in other words. (Which works out neatly from a romance point of view.)

But there's an implication to keep in mind: having your hero prose on about his feelings will subconsciously strike your readers as unrealistic. You should especially avoid this in the bedroom. When a guy is really turned on, he's not writing sonnets to his partner's eyes, because his blood supply is somewhere other than his brain. If you have him spouting poetry during a love scene, the reader will subconsciously believe he's not that turned on. Keep his dialogue short and simple when your protagonists are making love.

First Impressions

Another key aspect of heightening your hero's desirability is the way you introduce him. They're not kidding when they say, "first impressions are important." You don't want to give your readers the idea your hero is weak, because they'll find him a lot less attractive. This can be tricky, since you also need to establish his internal and external conflicts in those first couple of chapters.

In an early draft of my paranormal romance, *The*

Forever Kiss, I had hero Cade McKinnon getting his butt kicked by the villain in the first chapter. Unfortunately, I quickly realized this made Cade look too much like a wimp. So I added a secondary villain for Cade to best earlier in the story, while saving my superhuman bad guy, Ridgemont, for the last climactic battle. I could then build the main villain up even more. Since we know the hero isn't a wimp, if he's worried about the bad guy, he must have reason to.

I dealt with a similar first-impression problem in an early draft of *Master of Wolves*. My hero, Jim London, is an artist, so in the first scene, I showed him painting a portrait of his best friend. But the friend is a bounty hunter, so he came off as sexier than Jim did.

I ended up junking that scene and writing one in which the hero helps his buddy arrest a bail jumper. Jim is still an artist, but that's not the way we first see him. Our initial view of him is as an adrenalin junkie and part-time bounty hunter, which is yummier.

But remember, dominant or not, a romance hero is first, last, and always a hero. His behavior may seem rough, perhaps even borderline nasty -- with men if not with women -- but he always has a good reason for what he does.

Dominants

If you have a sexually dominant hero playing bedroom games of bondage and submission, the rules are a little different. In fact, he may even physically discipline his lover as part of a consensual sex game.

I suggest establishing that the reason he plays those kinds of games is not merely because he enjoys them, but because he knows they're something the heroine craves.

You must make it very clear to the reader that

he's totally focused on meeting the heroine's sexual needs. Dip into his point of view frequently to show that he's carefully watching her reactions to make sure she's safe and just as aroused as he is. He must be exquisitely careful not to push her too hard or accidentally hurt her.

Not only is this the behavior expected of romance heroes, it's the way real life dominants are expected to behave in the BDSM (Bondage, Discipline, Sadomasochism) community. Doms must be concerned about the well-being of their submissive partners, because people can get seriously hurt playing these kinds of games.

Now, the Doms may *act* as though they don't care for anything but their own pleasure, but that's a pose. The first rule of BDSM is "Safe, Sane, and Consensual," and you would do well to adopt the same motto for your fictional Doms as well.

By the way, if you are interested in portraying the BDSM community, I suggest doing extensive research. You'll find a bibliography at the end of the book listing good sources of information.

I'll discuss playing on the edge in more detail later. But first, let's discuss the second part of the erotic romance equation: the heroine.

Chapter Four: The Woman of his Heart

Get The Story Moving

If the hero is the engine of your heterosexual erotic romance, the heroine is the driveshaft. Nothing works without her. The hero is only pumping his pistons without a good heroine (or hero in a M/M) to get the story moving.

When I surveyed my readers, I found they had very definite views on what they did and did not like in a heroine. Some of those views were contradictory, but everyone agreed she needs just as much development as the hero.

As one woman explained, "As far as I'm concerned, the heroine is there so that I can relate to the story through her. It's harder for me to do through the hero, especially if he doesn't get a chunk of the POV/narration."

Barbie Need Not Apply

Whether your hero is an Adonis or a little rough around the edges, all my readers agreed the heroine shouldn't be perfect.

"I like flaws, other than stupidity (she can make mistakes, but they can't be *stupid* mistakes). I don't like physically perfect heroines; I find them hard to relate to. A heroine should not have a tiny waist, *and* perfect, large breasts, *and* the face of Helen of Troy, *and* three college degrees, *and* 20/20 vision, *and*… well, you get the picture. I don't have the necessary vanity to 'read myself' easily into the head of Rocket Scientist Barbie."

This particular comment made me want to write a Rocket Scientist Barbie. I made her the heroine of *Master of Fire*. I kept her from being obnoxious by giving her a past as a former plump little girl with zero sexual self-confidence, a result of going to high school at the age of twelve. You can make damn near anything work if you motivate it well enough.

"A heroine should be human, flawed, and likable," another reader agreed. "She should be someone I could at least make friends with, if I couldn't be her. In New Zealand we have the phrase 'size 8 bitch' (size 8 being the smallest women's size, where the 'perfect' 36-24-36 woman would be wearing a 12), the kind of girl (they always are girls, I think, not women) you just can't like because she's better than you at everything and smug with it. I don't like heroines who would qualify under that category."

So readers don't want perfect. But what do they want?

"I prefer heroines who are like me," another wrote. "Bold, brash and in your face. She should be able to stand on her own, hold her own in a fight, be intelligent and adaptable. I don't really care for shrinking violets or wallflowers. The heroine doesn't have to be sexually experienced, but she should know her own worth and be aware of her sexuality, whether she does anything about it or not. I'm partial to clumsy brainiac heroines as well, as long as they don't scare too easily. I like heroines who don't NEED a man, and sometimes don't even want one. I want her to realize it's okay to let someone close and allow them to watch out for you, to protect you, and it doesn't make the heroine less capable or strong."

But strong or not, a heroine still needs to be feminine as far as her emotions go.

"I like her to be in touch with her feelings, or be able to consider them to understand them. She has to know when to be soft and warm, and when to be hard and cold. She has to have a sense of humor. She has to be approachable, and be fair. And she has to have, or learn to have, confidence in her sexuality."

Another reader made an excellent point about creating independent heroines.

"I prefer heroines who could exist separately from the hero if they wanted to or had to -- therefore the choice to be together is truly a choice. I don't like heroines who "need" the man to complete them in the sense of being able to live in the everyday world."

She went on to add that if the heroine is obviously in over her head, turning to a powerful man for help is okay.

When you look at that flurry of strong opinions, it's intimidating. How do you do all that?

The consensus is she shouldn't be perfect in every physical characteristic. Personally, I write beautiful characters -- that's part of the fantasy for me -- but they don't see themselves as beautiful.

Actually, I'm not sure hot actresses sees themselves as physically perfect. I suspect they don't like their noses or thighs or breasts, because all women harbor a neurotic streak when it comes to appearance.

So if you want to write a beautiful heroine, make her hung up about some part of her body. Or, conversely, establish that she doesn't consider her looks particularly relevant to what she has to do. Perhaps her beauty is even a hindrance, because it keeps people from taking her seriously. She should not be obnoxious about winning the genetic lottery.

But no matter what she looks like, she needs some area of deep insecurity -- some fear or problem that consumes her. To be a strong, three-dimensional character, she's got to have an internal conflict -- *not involving the hero* -- that she must overcome over the course of the book.

In *Jane's Warlord*, my heroine had to overcome the sense of inadequacy her father had instilled in her. She ultimately does this when she confronts the villain. I often let the heroine administer the coup de grace to the villain -- after the hero has softened him up by beating the daylights out of him. Modern readers won't stand for a 1960s-style heroine -- the kind who stood back and wrung her hands and screamed while the hero was fighting for his life. Readers expect a heroine to have the physical courage to fight for her man and her children.

Balancing The Scales

Creating a heroine who is an equal to your hero can be a bit tricky, especially when he's superhuman to begin with.

When I was working on the idea for the Mageverse, the core idea was the men were vampires with a taste for women called "Latents." The women wouldn't become vamps. But that bothered me because it put them in a subservient position to the guys.

So I restructured the idea so that the women were magic users, and the men were physically powerful. The vamps need the women to work spells for them. In fact, the witches are so powerful, they can kill vampires and hold more power among the Magekind. That adds tension, because the vamps sometimes resent these powerful women.

Any time you can add conflict to a story, do it. It never fails to make the story stronger.

Kick-Ass Heroines

When the responses to my questionnaires started coming in, I was fascinated by how many strong, wide-ranging opinions my readers had on certain topics.

One of the most contradictory was their attitudes toward "kick-ass" heroines. Some readers love them, while others positively loathe them.

"I REALLY hate the kick-butt female, AKA 'Man in a Dress,'" one fumed. "I can't identify with her. This REALLY pisses me off in a story, to the point I won't read it if I see anything about her fighting off three dozen attackers while doing back flips."

"I find Buffy to be a cartoon and Laura Croft to be, well, a bigger, MALE cartoon," another agreed. "All they are (is) men with female parts... the feminine side is buried as being a negative."

Other readers, however, were in strong disagreement.

"A heroine needn't be a gung-ho marine kill 'em all dead type or the quintessential don't-need-no-man bitch, but I expect her to stand up for herself, use whatever her skills are to try to get herself out of a situation, be willing to accept help where necessary, and know when it's time to back down. What women might lack in physical strength, they more then make up for in native intelligence and cunning, so use it. That probably all goes out the window if your heroine is a shifter or vamp though, then you can get away with all the gung-ho killing you like."

"Agreed," another wrote. "I don't think she needs to be the ultimate in fighters... but I really doubt most women that have lived have been unable to defend themselves in a situation that required it. Personally, though, in cases of a more aggressive heroine, it'd be nice to see her rely more on tactical defense than physical."

Some readers liked kick-ass heroines because they make a nice change of pace.

"I get sick of heroines that faint at the sight of

blood, feel guilty to the point of vomiting if they kill in self-defense, etc. I'm not saying violence is good, but there's no one in this world that can convince me every woman/heroine should be pure of heart/spirit. A "kick ass" heroine is usually the opposite (okay, so not QUITE -- one day, I WILL read of an ambiguous heroine that does good and EVIL). The desire fueling that isn't about women-should-be-men but about the assumption that women are a certain way, and can't be any other way (I mean spiritually, etc --not physically). I figure there's too much diversity for that."

I think the key to pulling off these heroines is giving them a strong sense of femininity. Nora Roberts's Eve Dallas, for example, is a very sensual woman who is passionately in love with Roarke, her Irish billionaire.

Her neuroses help. Eve has a fear of her flamboyant hairstylist, Trina, and she's not terribly comfortable with girly trappings. These scenes also make for great comic relief in books that are often very dark.

Too, Roberts wisely makes Eve more than a little screwed up. She had a horrific childhood; her father was an abusive bastard she ended up stabbing to death when she was only eight years old. She's still haunted by nightmares about him. Roarke has a similar past, and Roberts uses that to bind the two characters together. They're damaged people who make each other stronger, but they're not supermen.

Sex And The Erotic Romance Heroine

All the preceding points apply just as well to any romance as erotic romance. But in erotic romance, you must deal with the heroine's attitude toward sex.

We expect men to be willing to bang anybody,

anywhere, anytime. But women, generally, are expected to have more caution, because the stakes are so much higher for us. After all, we're smaller than men, we're weaker than men, and we get pregnant. Not only that, but there are plenty of really sick men out there who get off abusing women.

So having your heroine pick up your hero in a bar and bang his brains out in the first chapter may not be a smart thing to do. Regardless of whether you consider that a moral thing to do, there's the issue of simple common sense. He could be a serial killer or an STD carrier for all she knows. Having sex with somebody like that falls under the heading of being Too Stupid To Live, which is not a characteristic we want in a heroine.

Unless, of course, you motivate it. Maybe your heroine has a death wish because this is the fifth anniversary of her child's death. You can get away with virtually anything if you can come up with a good enough reason for the character doing it. "I'm horny," however, is not it.

On the other hand, we do need her to go to bed with the hero early on in an erotic romance. I've been known to put love scenes in the second chapter of novellas.

The key, as in everything else, is to motivate the heroine's sleeping with this stranger. Something in her situation makes it necessary for her to do this.

Diana London, heroine of *Master of the Moon*, is a werewolf in heat who is struggling to control her dangerous impulses. Hero Llyr Galatyn is a Sidhe, meaning that for her he's a safe sexual partner. She can't infect him with lycanthropy.

In *Master of the Night*, Erin Grayson is a government agent who suspects Reece Champion of being in league with terrorists. She's wrong, but in the meantime, she decides to let him seduce her in order to get the evidence she needs to take him and the terrorists down.

In "Claiming Cassidy," in the *Mercenaries* anthology, Cassidy Vika sleeps with the hero even though he's an enemy warrior. He's captured her, and she's trying to get him to drop his guard so she can kill him and escape.

In each case, I had to establish that my heroine had very good reasons for what she did so she didn't come off as either a slut or a fool.

You also need to address her sexual history. She must be comfortable enough with her sexuality that it's believable that she'd make love to her hero so soon. That's why a virgin would probably be a bad choice for this kind of book, though I can think of ways to motivate it. Maybe she knows she's been earmarked as a virgin sacrifice for a woman-eating monster. With a motivation like that, the reader would forgive her for not being all that picky.

Still, outright promiscuity may not a good idea.

"I don't want the heroine to sleep with too many people," one of my readers wrote. She then went on to discuss two different books in which the heroines have sex with a number of men, observing that it worked in one book but not the other. "So it's a question of appropriateness, to the world and the characters already created."

On the other end of the spectrum, one of my readers said she hated virgin heroines and found them unbelievable, at least in contemporary romances.

Another, however, did not agree. "You know, I'm not at all bothered by the virgin thing. This is because the alternate choice is ALWAYS one of two things. Either the woman has disastrous (or just plain BLAH) encounters, or she sees men as boy toys there for her pleasure… and then she meets the hero and he's the most spectacular she's ever had… I get sick of it. I pretend the women didn't ACTUALLY think such things. I'm of a younger generation, so I've met a few women/girls my age that have had erotically successful relationships WITHOUT bed hopping. The fact that there isn't a single heroine that comes immediately to mind… is sad. Why can't a heroine have had a relationship that involved love and really hot sex, but eventually both decided friendship was the best choice for them, no bitterness about it for either party? I could almost think such things were for the ego of men (Oh, Master, you're the BEST I've ever had), but the books are geared toward women… At least a virgin has an excuse for that line."

In short, I think that you have latitude in creating your heroine, but you must motivate her, give her weaknesses as well as strengths, and make her a basically well-rounded character.

But don't be afraid to make her a little bit different too.

As one of my readers wrote, "I'm not saying that we need to go back to the old stereotypes of vapid virgins, Big Booby Bimbos, of Donna Reeds and June Cleavers or damsels in continual distress. What I am saying is that we should simply allow all types to exist… and that all types are not a neat package of expected or consistent behaviors. A woman can be tough, a great mom, a fierce protector, a fiery lover and still not be able to open a jar of pickles. Such is life."

Chapter Five: The Man of their Nightmares

Enter the Villain

If the hero drives the eroticism of your romance, it's the villain who drives the external conflict. The bad guy always gets the first move in his chess game with your couple. He sets off the action by trying to kill your heroine, by sending a threatening letter, murdering a schoolteacher, bombing a building -- whatever. The hero and heroine then must stop him.

Now, that's not to say you've got to have a classic villain -- a serial killer or drug runner or evil Sidhe king. Your villain could just as easily be your hero's mother, who wants her boy to marry her best friend's pretty daughter, or your heroine's boss, who pushes her to get the big account.

In fact, your hero and heroine are each other's antagonist -- standing between the character and what they want. That's what a good romantic conflict *is*.

But whoever the villain is, his role in the story is to make the protagonists work their behinds off -- and make the reader sweat. Will the protagonist catch the murderer? Will hero 1 overcome hero 2's objections to marrying him? Those questions keep the reader flipping pages.

Now, to generate all that tension, your antagonist must be more powerful than the protagonists, at least when the story starts. You've got to make the reader wonder how they're ever going to defeat the bad guy.

That can be tricky in a story where the antagonist is more pain in the butt than anything else, as in a romcom. You have to find a way to raise the stakes. Something major must be riding on the conflict -- if not life or death, then happiness or misery. Otherwise, there are no consequences if the protagonists lose. The higher the consequences, the more the reader sweats.

And there must be a very good reason why the protagonist has trouble dealing with the situation.

For example, the problem with the matchmaking mama plot I mentioned is that readers would expect a grown man to have the guts to tell his mother to stay out of his personal life. For that conflict to work without turning your hero into a wimp, his mother's displeasure must have consequences. Just the threat of her nagging the daylights out of him is not good enough.

Maybe she'll disown him if he doesn't marry her idea of the perfect daughter-in-law. In any case, she needs to have him over a barrel in a way that does not emasculate him.

If you are doing a more classical villain, you have it a little easier when it comes to structuring your external conflict. Maybe the villain is a cunning serial killer whose strength is that we don't know who he is, but we've got to find out before he claims his next victim. Maybe he's a Darth Vader type, big and scary and powerful, or an evil genius like Lex Luthor who can think rings around the hero. But in any case, the first encounter with the villain needs to be a decisive loss for the hero.

In a wonderful audio workshop called "Story Magic," Robin Perini states that when the story begins, the protagonists should be completely unable to beat the villain. It's only by learning and growing throughout the story that they become capable of winning in the end.

Constructing The Perfect Villain

Your antagonist also must be every bit as well-developed and three-dimensional as your heroic couple. Otherwise, he'll turn cheesy on you and infect your entire story with the scent of Limburger.

He needs to believe he's got a perfectly good reason for everything he does. And "I'm evil" is not it. True, the vampire bad guys in *Buffy the Vampire Slayer* were prone to announcing that hey, they were evil -- but most villains don't see themselves in that light. In their own eyes, they're the hero of the story, no matter how many murders they commit. Everybody else simply has it coming.

For example, the villain in *Master of Wolves* is driven by a need for power, but not for the usual reason. She was the victim of childhood sexual abuse at the hands of her wealthy grandfather, who told her powerful people can do whatever they want. So she grew up wanting power because it was the only way she'd ever feel safe.

However, I don't think she ends up being a truly sympathetic villain, because she's so matter-of-fact about the horrific things she does to get the power she craves. She feels no hesitation, no sympathy for her victims. She's a true sociopath.

It's also a good idea to give your antagonist a set of flunkies. You can have your protagonists kill off a couple to add to their street cred when they're otherwise getting their behinds kicked by the main villain.

Besides, the greater the numerical odds against your couple, the higher the tension for the reader.

Better still, give the flunkies different agendas, so they're in conflict with each other and the villain as much as with the hero and heroine. Any time you can get lots of different factors in play, you create tension as we wonder who's going to do what to whom.

Remember that unintended consequences can

always add a little nasty fun. For example, in *Master of Wolves*, the hero and heroine ambush the werewolf villain. They almost manage to kill him, but he escapes.

However, it's not good to let a heroic couple get a big win that early, so I had to figure out how to turn it against them. I decided that the near-defeat was the catalyst to make the villain decide he needed a pack of werewolves of his own. He promptly goes out and infects six other people with lycanthropy, so instead of being outnumbered two to one by my couple, he's suddenly got *them* outnumbered three to one.

In any given situation, consider what your antagonist's goals are and decide how they'd react to whatever the protagonists are doing. Have the villain escalate the stakes, getting more and more deadly with every encounter, so the situation gets worse and worse for our heroes.

By the way, if you're doing a serial killer or otherwise particularly nasty villain, make judicious use of the fade to black. If he's murdering helpless women with an axe, for God's sake don't show every blow. It doesn't advance the plot to show the poor victim's torturous death. Show just enough to demonstrate to us why we should be terrified of this guy, particularly if he later captures the hero or heroine.

Then do a judicious cut, showing the hero and heroine standing over the victim's body while you let the reader's imagination fill in the blanks. Otherwise, they may put the book down, especially if they think you've gone too far.

When you *are* dealing with a captured protagonist, it's okay to linger on their fear and helplessness, because that's important to the plot. Besides, the reader knows the lead is going to win and get away.

Which brings me to villains and rape.

If you've spent the book setting this guy up as a psychopathic serial rapist, and he captures the heroine, it's obvious what he's going to do next. *Don't let him do it.* I don't care what you have to do -- make sure the villain does not rape the heroine. The hero rescues her, she gets away, or somebody interrupts. *Get her out of there.*

That's vital for several reasons. From the standpoint of sheer story mechanics, if your heroine becomes a rape victim, she's not going to be emotionally healthy enough for a romantic relationship with the hero. Readers know she's going to be traumatized for a long time, and if you play her any other way, they'll be turned off. You'll lose all believability. More to the point, this generation doesn't want to see rape portrayed as entertainment.

Last but certainly *not* least, those scenes can be intensely triggering for women who have suffered rape in real life. Speaking as someone who once escaped a violent rape by the skin of my teeth forty years ago, I'd put a trigger warning on a book like that.

It's true that the *threat* of rape at the villain's hands can be intensely powerful and dramatic. Still, trigger warnings are your friends. Some people sneer at trigger warnings, but I view those people as lucky they don't know how bad PTSD from rape can be. That's a privileged attitude you can lose all too easily.

Mind you, I once had a reader tell me she was disturbed by the fact that my heroines encountered the threat of rape so often. She had a point, and I've steered clear of that plot device ever since.

I strongly recommend that you handle the issue with great delicacy too.

Chapter Six: Secondary Characters

Best Friends, Flunkies, and the Pizza Delivery Man

No man is an island, and neither are your main characters. They have people in their lives, whether mothers, fathers, brothers, friends, employees, or hit men. Their relationships with those people tell readers a great deal about who your characters are and what's important to them.

Secondary characters can range from walk-ons -- the guy who delivers the pizza -- to the protagonists' parents. Even people who never show up on the page can be profoundly important. Jane's abusive father appears in *Jane's Warlord* only in a couple of very brief flashbacks, but his presence looms. He's the heart and soul of her internal conflict about Baran and Druas, the villain. By defeating Druas, Jane symbolically defeats her father, something she was never able to do when he was alive.

So give a lot of thought to your protagonists' parents, siblings, employers, coworkers, and friends.

Devil's Advocate

Secondary characters also serve other important roles in the plot. Pure introspection -- the character thinking about his conflict -- tends to be one-dimensional and dry. It's much better if he has a best friend he uses as a sounding board, one who can either serve as the voice of reason or plant doubts about the romance. A good, rip-roaring argument is always more dramatic than five pages of navel gazing.

In *Master of Swords*, one of my heroine's best friends, Diera, just happens to be the hero's ex-lover. I use her to reveal that Gawain has a love-'em-and-leave-'em history. She's still bitter about the way he treated her. But just to make things interesting, I added another best friend to the scene: Caroline, whose attitude is completely different.

"Your assignment with Gawain concerns me."

"Oh, not you too!"

Caroline propped her chin on her fist. "You mean somebody else has been sticking her nose in your private life?" *(This little dig at Diera signals a conflict coming between the two friends.)*

"Yeah, only it's a him. Tristan." She told them about her great-grandfather's warning.

"He's got a point, Lark," Diera said. "Don't read too much into whatever you and Gawain have going on. Yes, he's handsome and charming, and Merlin knows he's skilled, but he's not interested in more than a night or two. You definitely won't be getting a Truebond out of him." *(Author's Note: A Truebond is the Magekind's answer to marriage.)*

The bitterness in her voice made Lark's brows climb. Caroline gasped exactly what she was thinking. "Ohmigod. You and Gawain had a thing!"

Diera shot her an exasperated look. "When

you've been around as long as we have, everybody has had a 'thing' with everybody else. And everybody knows it."

Caroline rolled her eyes. "Avalon -- the biggest small town in either universe."

Ignoring her, Diera turned an intense gaze on Lark. "Have you ever wondered how Kel stays alive? Obviously, he can't eat -- he's a sword." *(This bit is a piece of vital exposition I needed to slide in. Secondary characters are great messengers for this kind of thing.)*

Lark blinked, taken aback by the abrupt conversational detour. "Well -- I assumed he absorbs energy from the Mageverse."

Diera shook her blonde head. "He and Gawain have a symbiotic relationship. He draws on the knight's life force."

Caroline whistled soundlessly. "In other words, Gawain is eating for two."

"Exactly. Which means that unlike most of the other Magi, he can't subsist on bottled blood. He needs the psychic charge from taking it directly from a woman during sex. And he's never had a problem getting it."

Caroline grinned. "So you're saying if he were mortal, he'd have, like, six thousand STDs. Talk about a Magic Johnson."

Lark groaned at the pun. "You should be

ashamed."

Her grin broadened. "It's a gift."

Secondary characters are a great way to communicate necessary information -- but only if the protagonist doesn't know the facts already. In other words, don't have Mr. Spock explain warp drive to Captain Kirk. "As you know, Captain..." If he knows, Spock has no reason to tell him.

You can also have a good argument between two knowledgeable characters that lets the reader infer the details. It can be tough to make the exchange sound natural while giving the needed information, but you can pull it off.

Humor

Humor adds an important dimension in fiction, especially in an otherwise grim and gritty story. If things get too dark, readers may get so depressed they'll go off and read something more cheerful -- like somebody's obituary. Sneaking in the occasional laugh can lighten things up just enough to keep your readers engaged.

Secondary characters are perfect for this job, since they can get away with more outrageous behavior than your protagonists. You don't have to worry about making them look silly.

For example, Freika, my cyborg talking wolf in *Jane's Warlord*, gets all the best lines. I used him as badly needed comic relief from the main plot's serial murders.

You smell like sex, Freika commed to Baran

as they watched Jane bustle around the kitchen. *Why don't you look happier?*

It takes more than sex to make humans happy, Freika.

Which pretty well sums up your whole problem. The wolf flicked his left ear lazily. *You all think too much. If you thought less, you wouldn't make yourselves so miserable.*

Baran's lips curled in a wry smile. *You've got a point.*

Freika nodded regally. *Of course.*

Jane walked over and plopped a bowl down in front of his paws. "Breakfast is served. You ate the ribeye, so it's hamburger for you until we can go shopping."

He sniffed the bowl. "There's not enough meat in there to keep a Chihuahua alive."

"Yeah, well, I didn't expect to have the Big Bad Wolf for a houseguest. That's what you get when you drop in on people unannounced."

Suddenly something furry shot past to leap on the kitchen counter. Baran whirled, automatically dropping into a combat crouch.

Only to find himself almost nose to nose with a tan and black house cat. It meowed loudly, looking neurotic. Chagrined, he straightened.

"Perhaps I'll just have an appetizer," Freika said, eying the animal.

"Touch my cat and die, hairball." To her pet, Jane added, "Where have you been all night?"

"Hiding under the couch." The wolf took a fastidious bite from his bowl. "She's lucky I didn't just flip it over and snack." To Baran, he added, "And you say I have no self control."

"Leave the cat alone, Freika."

"Certainly -- if Jane starts buying a better cut of meat."

She looked up from operating something astonishingly loud; Baran's comp identified it as a can opener. "Keep it up and you'll be munching on the cheapest kibble I can find." Dumping the can's smelly contents into a bowl on the counter, she added to the cat, "Here ya go, Octopussy. Can you believe these guys? They think just because they come from the future, they get to eat us."

Baran grinned. "I didn't hear you complaining last night."

"You caught me in a weak moment."

Giving characters a sense of humor always makes them seem more believable and three-dimensional.

Once And Future Heroes

Secondary characters are also a good way to introduce future heroes in forthcoming books. Readers adore series, in part because they give writers a chance to show what happens in the lives of heroes and heroines from previous books.

Caroline, the best friend from *Master of Swords*, was the heroine of "Galahad" from the *Bite* anthology. I loved writing Caroline because of her snarky sense of humor, which made her perfect for the role of Lark's confidant.

Besides, I wouldn't mind a bit if readers who like her in *Master of Swords* go looking for her first appearance in *Bite*.

You can also set up a hero or heroine you plan to use in a future book. Jim London, hero of *Master of Wolves*, first appears as Diana's brother in *Master of the Moon*. I deliberately established Jim as a sexy Alpha male in the first book, and sure enough, readers started clamoring for his story.

Don't be surprised, though, if they also write in wanting a novel about secondary characters who are completely unsuitable for their own books. You'd be amazed at how many people asked me to write a romance for Freika. This dumbfounded me, since Freika is a wolf -- and not the kind who can shape-shift. There's no way I could write a romance around him. Besides, who the heck wants to read about wolf sex? I certainly don't want to write it!

Though in the final book of the trilogy, I did give

him a friend -- a cyborg talking horse.

I've even had people request a romance about Jane's dead mother, who appears in one flashback and is never seen again. They wanted to find out what happened to her, though I thought it was obvious: Jane's father killed her.

Given that experience, when I decided to write another sidekick character -- Kel in *Master of Swords* -- I set him up so I could use him as a hero later. Kel is a shape-shifting dragon who has been turned into a sword, but by the end of the book, he's free and in human form. He goes on to become the hero of *Master of Dragons*.

Be careful not to let your secondary character take over the book, though. Keep the focus on your hero and heroine. If the reader becomes more interested in a minor character, she'll be tempted to skim, looking for that character's next scene. But the book isn't about that character.

You need to give the primary characters enough conflict and great dialogue that the reader wants to know what happens to them, not dotty Aunt Gertrude. Aunt Gertrude, after all, is just the comic relief.

Secondary Romances

When you're writing a 100,000-word novel, you've got plenty of room for subplots. One of the best is a secondary romance that serves as a counterpoint for your primary couple's relationship.

In *Master of Swords*, Diera, Gawain's bitter ex-lover, ends up falling in love with her apprentice, Antonio. I used that romance to illustrate how a Truebond -- the Magekind's psychic version of marriage -- can have nasty consequences. This demonstrates the risk Gawain and Lark run when they

Truebond later.

It was a very sweet little tearjerker of a subplot, but I was careful to give it only as much page time as it needed. If you pulled it out of the book, it would be no longer than a short story. Otherwise, it might have diverted too much attention from Lark and Gawain.

If you find a secondary character or romance trying to take over, pull those characters out and give them their own book.

Tips For Dealing With Secondary Characters:

1. Minimize the number of minor characters in the story as much as possible. Readers find a flurry of names confusing, particularly in the first chapter.

2. If you have two jobs that need to be done in the story, have one character do them instead of two. For example, I needed someone to train my heroine in *Master of Swords*, so I used Tristan and Diera, two characters I'd already introduced.

3. Avoid having characters' names start with the same first letter. Readers will confuse them every time. That goes double for the protagonists and villain.

4. If a character is there simply to deliver pizza, don't give him a name and a detailed description. If you do make a point of giving a character a name, readers are going to expect him to recur, which, again, could cause confusion if he's just a walk-on.

5. If a character is significant to the plot, make sure you give him his own set of believable goals and motivations so he's not cardboard.

The better drawn your characters are, the more enjoyable your book will be.

Section Three -- Beginnings, Middles, and Endings
Structuring Your Plot

Chapter Seven: Begin as You Mean to Go On

Now that we've got our conflicts and our characters nailed down, it's time to start writing. Which means tackling the trickiest part of the book: the beginning.

Fiction's First Law: Show, Don't Tell

I once belonged to a writer's group in my hometown. During one meeting, I critiqued the work of a newbie writer who made some classic mistakes.

He started out with a rambling, confusing opening that managed to give me the impression the hero was a Forrest Gump type. I was startled to discover the protagonist was a teacher. Then he went on to reveal that this teacher had just learned his school was going to be closed and had decided to find out why.

Now, the basic plot idea could work, except the writer simply told the conflict without one scene or one bit of dialogue. You can't simply relate plot events as if you're telling somebody the story in a bar. You must show the events as they occur.

I tried to explain this, adding that the first two pages were really confusing.

"It was supposed to be," he told me. I gather he thought he was writing literary fiction, but what he was doing was shooting himself in the foot.

Every editor gets spammed with hundreds of submissions. Once a month or so, they take time off from their regular duties to read those emails. Most view this with all the enthusiasm of scrubbing bathroom grout. An aspiring writer only has the first couple of pages to catch that editor's attention before they go on to the next thing in the inbox.

My friend's attempt at literary artistry would have gotten rejected before the editor finished the first paragraph.

I tried to explain the first law of fiction to him: Show, don't tell. "Don't tell me about the conflict -- show it to me," I said. "Show me a scene about why the character cares that his school is going to be closed..."

"But he doesn't care," the writer interrupted. "He's just curious about why."

"If he doesn't care, why do you expect the reader to?" I asked. "You have to make me care, or I'm going to go off and read something else."

What this guy did not grasp is that nobody but his mother was going to read that book just so they could be impressed by his cleverness. Readers do not care how smart you are. They want to be entertained, and you need to show them in those first few pages that you're going to entertain them.

So how do you avoid that author's mistakes?

Sink Your Hook

I've already explained how to plan internal and external goals, motivations, and conflicts for your protagonists, and antagonist. Now you need to take that basic knowledge and decide how to use it to get your readers involved in the story.

The first chapter of a book is the most crucial, because it's the one that will determine whether anybody bothers reading the rest. In that initial chapter, you must establish your protagonists and their conflicts and make the readers care about what happens to them. They must be sympathetic, interesting people if you want the reader to spend the next 400 pages with them.

How do you do that?

First off, we care about people who care about people. If you show that a person loves his mother or his dog or his best friend, we're going to find him more sympathetic. Which means you can't show the character being a jerk without indicating that he isn't as bad as he appears.

I read a book in which the first scene was the hero discovering the heroine skinny dipping in a river. This is a classic romance scene, and it can make a yummy opening for an erotic romance.

Unfortunately, in this case the heroine and hero don't know each other, she's afraid of him, and he refuses to be a gentleman and leave. Instead, he leers at her.

I never got past the first scene.

For one thing, I'm a twenty-first century woman, and *I* wouldn't go skinny-dipping alone. What kind of Victorian virgin would be that stupid? Then the hero came off as a leering blackguard instead of a hero. So what this scene tells me is that this is a romance between a Too Stupid To Live heroine and a jerk. My life is just too short to read a book like that.

AK's Second Law applies: "You can't have an HEA with an asshole."

In case you're wondering, AK's First Law is, "When we have sex, we must all have the same number of legs."

When establishing your protagonists and their conflicts, you need to make sure that you don't end up portraying either so unsympathetically that you turn the reader off.

Sit down with your character's GMC and try to think of a scene that will show the protagonist's conflict in ten or so very tight pages. I usually do one such scene with the hero, and another for the heroine.

Then I do the meeting between the two.

You can also cut to the chase and show the meeting of the two characters first, but either way, you must show the reader that there's going to be lots of juicy fireworks ahead.

Even after all the books I've written, how to begin the newest one is always a challenge. For one thing, I like to create intricate paranormal worlds that can be difficult to explain. You don't want to drop a big honking brick of backstory in the first chapter for the reader to trip on. Yet you need to tell them enough that they know what's going on.

Here's how I introduced Gawain, the hero of *Master of Swords*.

* * *

Through a haze of red exhaustion, Gawain watched his rival reel and fall from his sword stroke. The last of his five opponents.

Thank Jesu. (One of the best ways to hook readers is to make them ask questions. This paragraph tells us Gawain has already defeated five opponents with a sword, which begs the question: why? Why fight five men? What's going on?)

He turned, his broken ribs screaming, and blinked hard, trying to free his eyelashes from the blood that tacked them together. Taking a step forward, he almost fell over one of the knights he'd defeated. Agony shafted up his thigh as he fought to regain his footing. His woolen breeches hung heavy and wet, and he knew the wound was responsible. (*This paragraph is designed to reveal core truths about Gawain. It shows us he's the kind of guy who has an iron will, who refuses to let pain and weariness keep him from his goals. Readers automatically sympathize with people who don't let suffering stop them. If I'd just said, "Gawain was the kind of man who didn't let anything stop him," it wouldn't have had anything like this kind of impact. That's the real meaning of "Show, don't tell" as a rule of fiction writing.*)

Cold. It was June, but he felt like the depths of winter. He'd lost too much blood.

A blurred ring of faces surrounded him. As he crossed the combat circle, their applause and cheers came to him as if from a great distance. A robed woman hurried past -- one of Merlin's newly created witches, intent on healing the men he'd bested.

No, not a witch, a Maja. They were called Majae now. He had to remember that. (*One of the challenges of world building is how to introduce the terms and ideas behind your world in an organic way. I could have explained the symbiotic relationship between Majae and Magi, but that would have taken several paragraphs and stopped the story in its tracks. You do not want to do that, especially in the first chapter. Never bore or overwhelm your reader right out of the gate. Tell them only what they absolutely need to know when they absolutely need to know it. Feed them in careful little bites, not great big plates.*)

Just as he was about to become a Magus. If the boy wizard found him worthy. Merlin had refused three other winners so far, though no one knew why.

He looked across the combat grounds to the two slender figures standing next to Arthur. Merlin and his lover, Nimue. To look at him, you'd think the wizard too young to shave, what with that narrow, thin face and stripling's body. At least until you looked into his eyes.

Something powerful and ancient looked out of Merlin's eyes, something far more God than boy. (*Merlin is an alien from a magical universe, but Gawain would have no way of knowing that at this point in the story. And in any case, it's more interesting for the reader if you let them wonder what the heck this guy is. Also note that I don't portray Merlin as that gray-bearded old man of the legend. That's yet another way to tell the reader that in my universe, the legends are wrong about almost everything.*)

Gawain took a step toward the wizard, but the world revolved around him, forcing him to stop in his tracks and grit his teeth. *I will not fall in front of him.* He'd endured too much to ruin it with weakness now.

Locking his gaze on the boy who was no boy, he dragged his right leg forward another step. And then his left.

Plop. Plop. Plop. The crowd had gone so silent as they watched his struggle, Gawain could hear the slow, steady drip of his own blood hitting the sand. (*Those kinds of sensory details make a scene pop off the page. And the fact that the plop is made by the hero's own blood gives it an extra kick.*)

Another step. And another. He seemed to be looking at Merlin through a long gray tunnel.

At last, thank Jesu, he reached his destination. (*If I've done my job, readers should be clicking the BUY button right about now.*)

Meeting Ms. Everywoman

By now, it's probably clear I write weird paranormal plots. This can be tricky, because if you throw a bunch of strange stuff at your readers, you run the risk of alienating and confusing them. They need someone in the story who views the events the same way they would, a kind of emotional lens who helps them understand what's happening.

In my books, that's often the heroine. She may be a werewolf, she may be a witch, but she's also, at base, an ordinary woman.

When I introduce her, I deliberately put her in a scene that shows her in the highest possible contrast to the hero. The reader immediately starts wondering how these two could ever become a couple.

Since I established Gawain as a skilled medieval warrior, disciplined and driven, I needed to show my heroine, Lark McGuin, in a different light.

* * *

Lark walked through the door of her tiny house feeling as if she'd been beaten. All day long, she'd fought to get food and water into her grandfather, who hadn't eaten in days. He'd met her attempts to feed him with a kind of sullen paranoia that told her more clearly than words that he had no idea who she was.

When Lark had tried to cajole one too many times, he'd lifted one big hand. He hadn't actually swung -- at least he hadn't fallen that far -- but she'd had no choice except to back off. (*Note the contrast between Lark and Gawain. He defeated five knights. She struggles to get her grandfather to eat.*)

Though eighty, her grandfather was six inches taller than she was, and he still outweighed her, if only barely. She'd taken care of him at home since he'd been diagnosed five years ago, but his growing belligerence had finally forced her to put him in the nursing home.

Now she collapsed on the sagging living room couch in a haze of exhaustion and worry. Long moments passed as she sat staring blankly at the fire chief's helmet that still held a place of honor on the coffee table. It was all she could do not to cry. (*That helmet is the symbol of her grandfather's past heroism. That's important, because Lark is driven by the need to live up to his example.*)

John McGuin had never once raised a hand to her growing up. If he'd been in his right mind, he'd be horrified at the idea of hitting any woman, especially his granddaughter. Alzheimer's had eaten away so much of his mind. It wouldn't be long before it finally killed his body too. (*This is Lark's motivation for what she does. She becomes a witch and takes part in a war she doesn't feel equipped to fight in order to save her grandfather.*)

Lark knew she needed to make herself a sandwich, knew she needed to keep her own strength up, but she didn't feel like eating.

Her heart ached. She missed her grandfather, and she was coming to hate the dying stranger in the nursing home. And she hated herself even more for wishing it was over. (*Gawain deals with physical pain in my intro of him, but Lark deals with emotional pain. The fact that she's driven by love and duty makes her sympathetic.*)

Convulsively, Lark rose from the couch and headed for the stairs. In her weariness, it felt as if her running shoes had turned to cement blocks. She kept going anyway. She had to do something, anything, no matter how insane. (*She does have something in common with Gawain. Both are heroic people.*)

She climbed up to the pitch-black attic and groped for the light bulb chain. A dull yellow glow clicked on, illuminating boxes of old records, clothing, and a pair of dusty stuffed poodles John had won her at the fair. (*These details were designed to contrast with the exotic medieval descriptions I used with Gawain.*)

It took her five minutes of searching to find the battered green footlocker. When she spotted it under a box of ancient Christmas decorations, she felt, against all reason, a spurt of hope.

This was nuts. She knew it was nuts. And yet… it was the only thing left to try. (*By this point, the reader should be wondering what's going on.*)

Kneeling on the dirty floor, Lark lifted the stiff, half-rusted lid and looked down into its sixty-year-old contents. Gently, she lifted out the folded Army uniform with its bloodstained cuffs, then pushed aside the Nazi flag her grandfather had captured somewhere in Normandy after D-Day. There, under a battered helmet, she found a long brown box and flipped it open. Stained white silk cradled two sharpshooter's medals, a colorful collection of combat ribbons, a Purple Heart, and a Bronze Star.

And a small, sword-shaped charm.

Lark took the charm out and returned the box to its spot in the locker. Closing a shaking fist tight around the charm, she closed her eyes and began the chant her Grandfather had made her say so many times when she was a little girl. The Gaelic words were difficult to pronounce, and she had no idea what they meant or if they'd do any good, but she said them anyway.

It was the only thing left to do. *(This is the point where we start edging away from the ordinary world.)*

When she was finished, she waited. The attic lay still and silent around her, filled with dust and the ghosts of childhood happiness.

Nothing happened. She hadn't really thought it would, and yet…

"Damn it, Granddad." Lark dropped her head on her fist and began to cry, first silent tears, then tearing sobs of grief.

Light flashed, so bright she saw it even through closed eyes. Her tears choked off as her head jerked up.

A shimmering hole had opened in the air. As Lark sat frozen in shock and dawning hope, a man stepped through it.

For some reason, she'd thought he'd be dressed in armor, not perfectly ordinary chinos and a blue knit shirt that matched his eyes. He cocked his handsome head as he looked down at her. "Hello." *(Again, I'm trying to play against expectations here.)*

Her mouth worked, but nothing emerged from her shocked vocal chords.

The man leaned down and… sniffed. "Definitely my lineage." *(The fact that he can tell that by smell shows us he's not human.)* He smiled as he straightened. "Are you John's daughter? I remember giving him that charm."

"G-Granddaughter." She stuttered it. Taking a deep breath, she blurted, "He needs your help."

Tristan smiled. "He has it."

First Encounters Of The Close Kind

Having engaged the readers' sympathy and interest in these characters, it's time to bring the protagonists together.

First, though, I threw another monkey wrench into the heroine's situation, by having her attacked by one of the bad guy vampires. He bites her, and she escapes death only by sheer luck. This shakes her confidence and leaves her with a fear of vampires.

And Gawain, of course, is a vampire.

* * *

Lark followed Gawain's broad back through the crowd. He was almost as outrageously handsome as Tristan, though his face was a bit more rough-hewn and angular. Blond brows matched the neat Van Dyke beard framing his mouth and the thick blond hair that lay around his broad shoulders. An embroidered tunic covered the kind of muscular chest only built by swinging a broadsword, and his dark hose clung to a pair of powerful horseman's thighs. Gleaming black boots sheathed his legs to the shin, adorned by a pair of golden spurs -- the symbol of knighthood. *(Here we're establishing Gawain's physical attractions.)*

Lark would have thoroughly enjoyed the view, if not for the sensual hunger glinting in Gawain's green eyes. After her run-in with Fangface the Sorcerer, she wanted to avoid vampires for a while.

That, however, wasn't really possible. Thanks to Merlin, Magi and Majae enjoyed a symbiotic relationship -- the vampires needed to drink the witches' blood, and the witches needed to donate it. Otherwise, a Magus would starve, while a Maja's blood pressure could spike so high, she'd suffer a stroke. *(This increases Lark's internal conflict even more; she has medical reasons to give blood.)*

Fortunately, you could bottle your donations, which is what Lark had been doing. She hadn't had time to look for a lover since becoming a Maja, since she'd either been out on missions or training with Diera and Tristan.

Come to think of it, Fangface had been only the second vampire who'd ever bitten her. *(Making her so inexperienced intensifies the conflict.)*

Lark's hands curled into fists. Presumably

Gawain wouldn't tear into her with Fangface's viciousness -- she'd actually enjoyed Dominic Bonnhome's vampire lovemaking, after all -- but still, just the thought of it made her break out in a cold sweat.

I'm so not ready for this.

But if she admitted she was afraid, Gawain would think her a coward. She'd grown up listening to firefighters joke about gutless rookies. She was damned if she was going to become the butt of that kind of joke.

John would be mortified.

Again, what I'm doing is stacking internal and external pressures on Lark, all centered on having sex with Gawain.

She does have sex with him in the next couple of chapters, but that conflict segues into the underlying problem: Lark's lack of confidence in her own abilities.

And that's the conflict that drives the rest of the book.

Chapter Eight: Man (and Woman)

The Middle

One of the favorite topics for *YouTube* videos on writing is how to avoid the sagging middle. For me, that's never been a problem. I've always set up the book's middle as the place where everything goes to hell. Then I stand back and watch the protagonists try to contain the damage and deal with the fallout. It's even better if their actions spur the villains into raising the stakes with more devastating attacks.

Note that the tension needs to ramp up so that each crisis is worse than the one before. This leads the reader to anticipate the explosive climax they crave.

Making A Bad Situation Worse

In the first six chapters of *Master of Wolves*, I established just how bad the situation is for Faith Weston, my cop heroine. Dead bodies are turning up ripped to pieces, and she begins to suspect somebody in her small-town police department is involved. Then she's bitten by the bad guy werewolf and endures the agony of her own transformation. Just before she turns, she learns that Rambo, her drug dog, is really a werewolf named Jim London. Jim suspects her entire department of involvement in his best friend's murder -- and he's right.

Over the seven chapters of the middle, I keep pouring gasoline over Faith's personal forest fire. The evil werewolf bites more cops. The witch gets her hands on a magical object called the Black Grail and turns the other cops into vampires.

Meanwhile, our badly outnumbered heroic couple is trying to prevent more deaths. At the same time, they must deal with the problems created by their growing mutual attraction. Faith isn't happy about being a werewolf, and she's not sure she trusts Jim, despite the simmering sexual attraction between them. Her experience with handsome men hasn't been good. For his part, Jim is frustrated because though they have toe-curling sex, Faith doesn't want to fall in love with him.

In a romance, love doesn't make things better, at least not initially. In fact, it generally tosses a hand grenade into a bad situation, making the external conflict you're supposed to deal with that much harder to resolve. It's not until the end of the book that we see love as a purely positive force in the characters' lives.

Turning Up The Heat

A key question to ask yourself when planning your middle is, "What's the worst possible thing that could happen to this character -- given their particular emotional hangups -- that they could still survive?"

Then do it to them.

For example, my fairy king in *Master of the Moon* is being stalked by magical assassins. Llyr has fantastic magical powers, but he still needs a cadre of Sidhe bodyguards. In the middle of the book, he loses his powers and his bodyguards are all killed. Suddenly Llyr can't defend himself or his heroine, Diana London. He must get those powers back.

You have to be merciless with your people. The more they suffer, the more the reader will both root for them and worry about them.

Love In Bloom

The middle is also where the romance begins to flower. Even as events all around them go straight to hell, the hero and heroine fall in love as the danger they face brings them closer. This has the effect of intensifying the sense of risk, because the characters now have more to lose.

And it's not just all about the sex, either. Bodies may inspire lust, but it's character that inspires love. You need a scene at some point in the middle where the hero suddenly sees the heroine in a new way: *Wow, she's something special. She's not like any of the women I've had before.*

Whether or not the character realizes it, that's the moment when he's a goner. What's more, the reader will recognize that moment and realize things are about to get seriously complicated.

Here's the scene from *Master of the Night* in which vampire Reece Champion realizes he's in love with Erin Grayson:

> After almost three hundred years, Reece had finally met a woman he could love. And the odds were very good he'd end up destroying her.
>
> The bitterness of that knowledge gnawed at him even now, as he lay with Erin sprawled on top of his body, limp with sated pleasure, the taste of her blood in his mouth. His cock was still inside her, though he could feel it slipping slowly out as it softened. *(I used these sense details to build the sense of loss and regret.)*
>
> She deserved so much better than this.
>
> He thought of the women he'd known and enjoyed over more than two centuries as a

vampire. Mortals and Latents and Majae, the beautiful and the brilliant, the courageous and the honorable and the skilled. Erin had it all, wrapped in one luscious package that managed to arouse both his lust and his admiration.

Damn, he didn't want to do this to her.

If the Change went bad, that wonderful mind would crack under the Mageverse's psychic battering, and he'd have to kill her. Even if she proved strong enough to withstand the sudden acquisition of all that power, if she couldn't break them out of the cell, Geirolf would return and kill them both. (*This is love turning the screws with a vengeance.*)

Well, no, Reece realized, as his heart sank. He couldn't allow her to be used that way. He'd have to kill her himself. (*And I tighten those screws even more.*)

Their only chance -- and it seemed slim -- was that Erin could use her power to break them free. And even that was a dicey proposition, because they could easily end up facing a death sentence from the Majae's Council. True, the witches would probably understand, given the seriousness of the situation with Geirolf. But the Majae could be a capricious lot, and he'd learned long ago he couldn't always predict what they'd decide.

All they needed was for someone to have a vision indicating Erin was dangerous, and they'd end up facing a Round Table execution team. *(Again, I keep coming up with ways to make the situation as bad as possible. Even if they escape one trap, there are others waiting in the wings.)*

Not that any of that mattered one way or another. Reece was committed to Changing her now, regardless of the outcome. And he'd been in combat often enough to know that if you concentrated on the fact that you were probably going to die, you were virtually guaranteed to do just that.

The thought of his own death didn't really bother him. He should have been dead centuries ago; he could hardly bitch about the hand he'd been dealt now. But Erin was a different story.

If the next couple of hours were all she would ever have, he was damn well going to make them good ones. Starting right now. *(This gives Reece a chance to demonstrate his new love to Erin and the readers. This being erotic romance, he's going to do it with a love scene.)*

I structured *Master of the Night* to ensure that each sexual encounter has real importance to the plot.

The reader learns that if Reece and Erin make love three times, she may gain the power to free them from their enchanted cell. On the other hand, she may go insane from the magical cascade, forcing Reece to kill her.

Thus, every time they make love, the tension increases. One way I do this is by having Reece fight making love to her at first, as he desperately tries to find another escape route.

That third explosive love scene builds to Erin's frantic attempt to free them -- an attempt that appears to fail until Reece uses the weakness she's created to break them out. Then I up the stakes again by having Erin so drained, she's on the verge of dying.

You need to set up your own book along similar lines. Make the sex count. Ensure it serves a purpose in the plot. At the very least, your love scenes should give the hero and heroine a respite from all the angst and tension generated by the external conflict. The reader needs that respite, because as the book heads to its climax, things are about to get seriously ugly.

Chapter Nine All's Well that Ends Well

The last quarter of your book is the build-up toward the end. By now, all the problems and conflicts you've created for your couple are reaching critical mass. All hell is about to break loose, and your characters know it.

More importantly, so does the reader. And she can't wait to find out how you're going to save your couple from disaster.

The Emotional Climax

In the following section on action, I'll describe how to resolve the external conflicts between your couple and your villain. But first, you must engineer an emotional climax as your couple confronts their inner demons.

In *Jane's Warlord*, for example, my heroine must overcome her fear and face the murderous serial killer, Druas. Baran gives her a ring that will disable the protective armor Druas wears so the hero can defeat him.

> She turned and moved quickly to the night stand to open the drawer. Her father's gun lay inside, loaded and ready. For once, the weapon was a comfort instead of a symbol of doubt and fear.
>
> Hearing a tread on the stairs, Jane pulled out an old romance novel and slid the drawer partially closed.
>
> *I'm not going to throw up*, she told herself fiercely. *I can do this. All I've got to do is rest*

the ring against his suit for just a second. I can do that.

You're going to die, her father's ghost hissed.

Fuck you, Daddy. (*This demonstrates that by working with Baran, she's learned to trust herself.*)

The bedroom door opened. Baran walked in. But he'd just stepped into the closet...

For just an instant, Jane was confused. Then it hit her. It was Druas. The son of a bitch was using his imagizer to look like Baran. He thought the Warlord was still back at Tom's house, as the report Tom would falsify would claim he was.

The killer smiled Baran's smile at her. "I decided you were right. I'd never be able to convince the detective I didn't do it. Taking him hostage was a mistake."

Suddenly Jane's fear was gone, washed away by pure rage. The bastard was playing a game with her, planning to use her love for Baran against her. (*Here we see love finally at work as a strengthening force. It gives her the courage to stand up to Druas.*)

For once, years of hiding her emotions from her abusive father stood Jane in good stead. Her face automatically fell into the sweet, doll-like smile she'd learned under Bill Colby's belt. (*Jane turns her experiences with her abusive father into a positive, another victory over his metaphorical ghost.*) "I'm glad you saw the light," she said. "Once Tom gets an idea into his head, you couldn't pry it loose with a crowbar."

"Yeah," Druas said in Baran's deep voice. He tried a smile of his own, but now Jane realized how unlike her lover's the expression really was. Evidently the computer used the expression he was actually wearing on the face of the protected image. The result was like looking at a perfect mask of the man she loved -- worn over the face of something cold and reptilian.

He moved closer to her. "I thought we might as well make use of what time we've got left together."

I'll just bet you do, you son of a bitch. But did he really want to have sex, or was he just trying to get close enough to kill her?

Either way, she had to play along just long enough to rest her hand on his chest until the ring disabled his suit.

If he didn't kill her before it could do its job. (*Here I'm pointing up the risk she's running.*)

Baran had never felt such rage in his life, not even when he heard Liisa's last scream.

The idea that Druas had dared to wear his own face while planning to murder Jane made him want to pound the killer to a bloody bag of shattered bone. He'd been about to drive right through the closet door when Freika had caught his hand in fanged jaws, jolting him back to his senses.

Now he crouched seething in the darkness, watching through the door slats and praying to all his people's gods he'd be in time to stop whatever Druas was planning.

He had to go to *riaat* at just the right moment. If he entered the berserker state too soon, he wouldn't be able to maintain it all the way through the battle; too late and he might not have the strength to save Jane when he needed it. *(This states in a nutshell the problem he's going to face when he fights Druas.)*

At least she was playing her role to the hilt. He'd been afraid that she couldn't control her justifiable terror. Yet the minute Druas had walked in, she'd gone icily calm.

Now she was smiling into the murderer's face, projecting seductive warmth, almost glowing with sensuality as she flirted, quite literally, with death. Even Druas looked fascinated. Despite his fear, Baran felt the rise of admiration mixed with a curious pride. A week ago, he would never have thought a civilian capable of such cool, brassy courage.

But then, Jane was no typical civilian. *(Baran has learned his lesson. Despite being a mere human, Jane is intelligent, courageous and capable.)*

He just had to make damn sure he was ready to snatch her clear when the killer made his move.

The Black Moment

The situation continues to get worse until it reaches what is called The Black Moment. That's the point when the protagonist thinks everything is lost, and they must make a final last-ditch decision that turns everything around.

In *Jane's Warlord*, that moment falls after Druas is dead, when Jane and Baran think they've won. That's when the temporal enforcement agent arrives to take Baran home, and everything goes straight to hell.

Again, this moment was born of a single question: What's the worst thing that could happen? Since Baran had been sent to prevent a time paradox that could destroy the universe, the answer was obvious.

Baran's strength is so completely drained after the fight, he can't even stand, much less defend Jane. He lies on the floor at the agent's feet...

"Well, you evidently lived up to your reputation, Warlord," the man began as

Jane gaped at him. His skin was an inky black with shimmering blue highlights that was not even remotely human. The darkness stood in stark contrast to the fiery shimmer of red curls tumbling around his ethereal face. "You've completely wrecked this…"

Then the man's metallic gaze fell on her, and he looked every bit as dumbfounded as she felt. "You're alive!" He took a half-step back. "You aren't supposed to be alive!"

"Shit," Jane said, clutching Octopussy so close the cat began to squirm. "I knew it."

Baran struggled to focus on the TE agent despite the hallway's slow revolutions around him. "What do you mean, she's not supposed to be alive? You told me…"

"You were supposed to try to keep her alive -- you weren't supposed to succeed!" The agent gave him a wild-eyed look. "You have to kill her now!" (*Again, I'm turning up the heat on my couple.*)

Baran looked at him, feeling even colder and sicker than he had a moment ago. "Fuck off."

Accurately reading his snarl, the Enforcer looked at Freika, who stood at Jane's side as she cradled Octopussy in one arm, the gun held awkwardly in the other hand. "Forget it," the wolf told him. "I wouldn't even touch her cat."

The Enforcer squared his shoulders, taking on a grim look. "Then I'll do it." He took a step forward.

Jane, standing on the other side of Baran, began to back up toward the stairs. Terror grew in her lovely eyes as she read the menacing intent in the agent's.

Hell, Baran thought. *Give me something, comp. I've got to…*

No reserves left. (He'd used them all up fighting Druas. I had to set it up this way, because I'd already established Baran could wipe the floor with this guy under normal circumstances.)

The Enforcer started to step across his sprawled body. *Never mind, I'll use what I've got.* He lifted one leaden hand, wrapped it around the agent's ankle. Jerked.

With a startled yelp, the Enforcer went down as Baran forced his drained body to roll onto hands and knees and scrabble after him. He didn't so much pounce on the agent as fall across him.

"What the hell are you doing, Arvid?" the Enforcer roared, struggling to escape as the Warlord wrapped his legs around his body and curled an arm across his throat.

"You're not killing her!" Baran gritted, glad the bastard didn't have sensors. Otherwise he'd know how close he was to passing out.

"Do you want to cause a paradox? She's got to die!"

Keep upping the tension like this, creating traps for your hero and heroine they can escape only by overcoming their romantic and emotional conflicts. The result will be a stunning, highly emotional ending that will have readers haunting bookstores in search of your next novel.

Tie Up Dangling Threads

Last, you should use your ending to tie up any dangling plot threads. Do not leave your readers with unanswered questions, because it drives them nuts. In *Jane's Warlord*, I never directly said that Jane's father killed her mother -- I thought it was self-evident, and Jane had resolved the conflict anyway. But I had several readers gripe about that plot point. If I ever get the chance to do an updated version of that book, I'm going to make sure to resolve it.

Another of the issues you must tackle in an erotic romance is whether the protagonists get married. In a novel, you've got to make that clear. You need that HEA.

In a novella, a proposal may not be believable because the couple have known each other such a short time. Yet in either case, my readers say they do want to know that the foundation for a permanent relationship has been laid.

"I don't need to know that they stay together

forever," one wrote, "but there has to be a good solid relationship at the end or else what's the point? I don't have sex just for the sake of sex, so why would I want to read that?"

Another agreed. "I've got to at least believe they have a chance at an HEA. And they've got to be happy with each other at the end. If something's left looming, it'd better not be their feelings for each other."

That said, some readers don't mind something more tentative.

"I'm also satisfied with a "Happy for Now Ending" where they're not sure if they'll stay together but they're willing to try and see how it works out for them," one wrote. "That type of ending feels more realistic for me because many times a successful marriage and relationship is determined by how they work out the good and bad over a long period of time, after the rush of the first love has faded. For instance, in J.D. Robb's *In Death* series, both hero and heroine are strong, opinionated characters who fight and argue at times, it's not all lovey-dovey between them but they work their differences out and make up in the end."

Yet, another reader said she was more interested in the right ending for the characters.

"Here's what I think of happily ever after: it's all relative," she wrote. "I prefer happy for now, especially in series works. However, it is relative both to the characters themselves and what's right for them and for the plot of the story. Although if an author is leading me to HEA then doesn't deliver, I get pissed off. You have to keep continuity and characterization in mind when writing an ending of any kind."

As I've said before: *keep your promises*.

Section Four -- Action
In and Out of Bed

Chapter Ten: Beyond BIFF and POW
Writing the Perfect Fight Scene

I decided to pair the chapters on writing sex and fight scenes in this section because I think they have a great deal in common. Both are action sequences in which emotions run high and sensation is paramount. True, the emotions and sensations are opposites: pain and fear in fight scenes, pleasure and love in love scenes.

Yet both kinds of scenes give writers a great deal of trouble for what amounts to the same reason: *fear*. With fights, writers fear being too violent and turning readers off. With love scenes, writers fear revealing too much about their own sexual selves. But in both cases, a writer is best served by holding nothing back. That's the key to delivering maximum emotional impact for readers -- and making sure they come back for more.

One of the most universally necessary skills for all genre writers is the ability to pen a good fight scene. Depending on the genre, you may never need to write a love scene -- and that includes in some kinds of romances, such as sweet and inspirational. Yet fight scenes are expected in everything from mysteries to science fiction.

That's particularly true for the climax, when readers want to see the bad guy get his comeuppance in some suitably humiliating and painful way. After all, this jerk has been making the protagonist's life miserable for at least 300 pages. We want our good guy to get a little payback.

If we don't get that longed-for catharsis... Well, result is an anticlimax, a sure-fire way to ruin a good book. I can't tell you the number of times I've been left disappointed and frustrated *because* some writer failed to pay off 400 pages of build-up.

Even very skilled romance authors sometimes drop the ball. Some published writers evidently have a lot of trouble writing fight scenes at all, despite working in romance sub-genres that call for them.

I believe there are a couple of reasons for this, and you'd do well to be on the lookout for them in your own work.

First is the belief that ladies don't fight. Fighting is dirty, and people sweat, and anyway, it's only fun until somebody loses an eye. Besides, the writer mumbles, "I don't like hurting people." So she lets her villain get hit by a bus.

But you're *not* hurting people, and you're *not* sweating or getting dirty. Your characters are. You've crafted this big, sexy Alpha male who bench presses twice his own weight and looks good in a ripped T-shirt. You need to be true to what this guy would really do in the situation you describe. The bad guy has just tried to blow up an elementary school, murdered your hero's best friend, stolen his woman and kicked his dog. Your hero is, at the very least, going to want to knock the villain's teeth down his throat while calling him very bad names.

Respect The Testosterone

Remember: your reader is a kind and gentle soul who loves children and dogs and never says a nasty word to anyone, no matter the provocation. In other words, she's *deeply frustrated*.

And after 400 pages of wanton villainy, she wants the hero to kick the bad guy's butt. Hard. Gentle Reader is a bloodthirsty little wench in the privacy of her own pages. Give her all the mayhem she craves, and she will love you for it.

Most of all, resist the impulse to let your villain get hit by a bus. Yes, it may be a messy and painful end, but for a satisfying climax, the protagonists must be directly involved in whacking the villain. Pushing the antagonist in front of the bus is a possibility, if not particularly heroic. Otherwise, we feel cheated.

A good rule of thumb is, whoever the villain hurt the most should have a role in killing him off or sending him to jail. Personally, I like death. I've seen the criminal justice system in action too many times.

As for the heroine, as I've said before, don't just have her standing on the sidelines wringing her hands. Get her involved. Even if she's an ordinary woman while both hero and villain are supermen, she needs to do something. She helps trap the villain or shoots him after the hero beats the snot out of him -- *something*.

By the same token, don't let your Alpha male stand on the sidelines while the heroine faces death. I've seen this done, and it's bad. He needs to be working his tail off to save her, even if she is a kick-butt heroine with superpowers of her own. *Heroes do not let women and children face danger without doing something about it.*

Book fatigue can also cause you to wimp out in your climax. Now, I was raised on *Star Trek* and *X-Men* comic books, and there's nothing I love more than a good brawl. Yet I must admit that after writing a book for months, with my deadline far too close and *THE END* in tantalizing reach, I have to fight the urge to rush the climax.

Let the book cool -- or come back from the initial edit -- and take a hard look at the ending. If it feels rushed, it probably is. Put in more details and spin it out a little longer to give it more punch.

Good Guys Vs. Bad Guys

What gives a book its power? It's not beautifully described sunsets, witty dialogue, or even kinky sex scenes -- it's *emotion*. Romances are all about emotion: the developing love between the hero and heroine.

But the dramatic foil -- that is, the artistic contrast -- for that developing love is the developing hate between the protagonists and villain. This serves as a sort of anti-romance that makes the romance shine brighter by contrast. The villain's brutality and selfishness emphasizes the heroes' love and self-sacrifice. The antagonist's machinations give them the opportunity to prove their love to each other and the reader. By standing up to him, the protagonists show they *are* heroes.

As I've said, villains drive the external conflict. The protagonists are minding their own business when the villain comes along and tries to murder them, forcing them to defend themselves.

That means your villain can't be a wimp, because a wuss antagonist means a limp conflict. If the bad guy is a 98-pound weakling who sends nasty notes to the heroine, the reader knows that as soon as your 200-pound hero gets his hands on the little jerk, he's going to pound him into paté.

So the villain must be more powerful than the protagonists, either physically or politically or because he's got his own personal army. Otherwise, the reader isn't going to worry, and a reader who isn't worried is one short step from bored.

Which is why nasty notes aren't enough. There must be a gun or a bomb or a case of anthrax in the plot somewhere -- something that puts our protagonists in real physical danger.

And make it personal. While you're developing the love story between the couple, develop the hate between them and the villain. The bad guy's desire to kill them can't be just business, even if it starts that way. By the end, they should all loathe each other with such consuming passion, the reader is deeply invested in the payoff.

It's even better if you can give the hero and villain some kind of history. Some jerk opening fire on a heroic cop will make us feel for the cop, because the cop is fighting for survival. If we know the jerk is also a serial killer who eats people, that's going to raise the stakes because this guy will kill again if he's not stopped.

But if the serial killer just ate the protagonist's sister, that's going to raise the stakes far more. And if the serial killer has kidnapped the heroine and is about to eat *her*, now we're cooking. (Pardon the pun.) We and the hero want this guy dead.

So the more personal you can make it, the better, especially if you build the conflict in repeated encounters during the book.

The Sensual Fight Scene

Just as the love scene illustrates the development of the romance, so the fight scene illustrates the growing hate and violence between your villain and heroes.

The fight scene may also be the only place the heroes and villain come into direct contact, so it's vital for developing the hate between them.

Just as in love scenes, you need to make sure you use all five senses on every page -- taste, scent, hearing, touch, sight. Give us the metallic taste of blood in the heroine's mouth, the reek of sweat and fear, the thunder of the gunshot, the staggering pain of a fist hitting flesh, the infuriating sight of the villain's triumphant smirk.

Go light on the dialogue. Resist the urge to have the protagonist and villain chat during a fight scene. It's not realistic. When people are really ticked off, they don't have the higher brain function for James Bond-style witticisms. All their focus is on staying alive. If they're chatting, it reduces the sense of danger, so keep the dialogue to a minimum. You can have them talk for a minute or two before the general butt-kicking commences, but afterward, keep it minimal.

Don't skimp on these scenes either. They need to be at least five to ten manuscript pages long to have emotional impact. As the book goes on, confrontations should get longer and more intense. The final fights in my books are usually twenty to thirty pages.

Like love scenes, each fight should come to some kind of climax. Generally, that means one or the other running for their lives, at least in the earlier fights. After all, you can't let the protagonist knock the villain off too soon.

Each fight scene should give the reader the sense that the stakes are increasing. The injuries get worse, the losses get more catastrophic. The more you increase the stakes, the greater the tension.

The last battle should have the greatest bang. Don't detonate an atomic bomb in Chapter Five, because you're not going to be able to top it in Chapter Twenty.

Location, Location, Location

When you're planning a fight scene, think about where you're having it, what time of day it is, and how this location is going to affect the fight. Is it a good place for the kind of fight you've got in mind?

I had a fight in a burning house in *Jane's Warlord*, but under ordinary circumstances, that's not a realistic location. It's pitch dark in a burning house, the smoke is so thick you can't breathe, and the heat will sear your lungs. I got away with it only because my hero and villain were superhuman.

I use the darkness, smoke, and heat to add to the tension. My hero must rescue a woman and fight past the villain before the victim's lungs are destroyed by the heat. This gives him a time limit, which is a great way to increase tension in any situation.

I've also used the time of day during fights. In *Forever Kiss*, my two vampires fight a duel in late afternoon (my vamps don't burst into flames, but they do suffer nasty radiation burns).

My hero is struggling with the heat, and at one point, he's blinded by the afternoon sunlight hitting his face. The bad guy almost takes his head, but Cade swings blindly and gets the villain first. This close call was designed to make the reader heave a sigh of relief. And since Cade is badly hurt in the fight, it also turns the screws at the same time.

How much room do you have to fight in? If it's a narrow stone corridor, you're not going to be able to swing a sword. The kind of moves you can do in your fight are going to be constrained, so both antagonists and heroes will want to find a better location.

Who has the advantage? Historically, if you've got the high ground in a fight, you can shoot downward at your attacker, over any cover they might be trying to hide behind. And if they're trying to charge up at you, they've got to work harder, while you can use gravity and momentum in your attack, making it easier to jump them.

Don't forget the innocent bystanders. A crowded

shopping mall gives your villain all kinds of prospective hostages to play with.

Trading Punches

Writing a fight scene may seem really daunting, but there's a certain logic to it. It's not unlike a chess game.

When somebody launches an attack -- whether by hand-to-hand, sword or gun -- there are only two options. You get hit or your opponent misses.

Now, you can make them miss by either blocking the attack or by dodging it. But when you see an attack coming at you, you *must* respond in some way before you do anything else. Ignoring the attack and launching your own will only get you killed.

After you've dealt with that attack, you must either make your own attack or retreat. Your foe, in turn, will either block or get hit.

In this way, you can write your way through a fight by reasoning out what each move should be.

I start out with an initial attack -- a roundhouse to the jaw, for example -- and then I figure out what the opponent's countermove should be. They could make a forearm block to knock the punch away, for example, or they could jerk their head back to avoid it.

Then I decide on the return attack. Ideally, the opponent needs to do something they think will take their foe out as quickly as possible. Fights are painful and exhausting, and you can get badly hurt in them. So you want to win in a hurry.

Maybe the character lands a kick on the outside of their opponent's knee in a blow designed to cripple. The opponent hits the ground with a howl of agony, and then promptly kicks our protagonist with the good leg.

It's important to mix up the moves like that. Just having the characters exchange punch after punch is boring, not to mention unrealistic.

Again, fights are painful. Your hands hurt, your body hurts, your muscles ache, you sweat and fight exhaustion. You break things, you sprain things, you get too tired to fight at all. Put yourself into the characters' POV as deeply as you can and try to describe how fighting feels -- the pain, the fear, the building exhaustion and desperation. Those emotions are powerful and will propel the reader to the edge of their seat.

Use every weapon at your character's disposal. Nobody, including heroes, fights fair when their lives are at stake. They're going to use fists, feet, teeth, fingernails, a butcher knife, a nail file -- anything and everything. Get creative.

Jane in *Jane's Warlord*, faced with Baran's overwhelming strength -- she thinks he's a serial killer at the time -- throws the contents of a bottle of perfume in his face. It's the only logical thing she can do, because he's vastly stronger and faster than she is. She has to be smarter. *The best weapon your characters have is their brains. Do the unexpected, and your readers will love you.*

Sword Fights

Anybody who thinks the pen is mightier than the sword never wrote a sword fight.

There's something romantic about a sword fight. Two men, meeting at dawn to duel over the honor -- or lack of same -- of a beautiful woman. Conflict, violence, sex and romance, all wrapped up in a neat little package no writer can resist.

However, you should know that there's a lot

more to fencing than two guys sticking each other with big shish kabobs.

First, there's the selection of weapons. People in the medieval age were as endlessly inventive in designing swords and knives as the Pentagon is in coming up with things that explode.

The design of swords changed a great deal over the centuries depending on the fighting styles and technology of each period. During the Middle Ages, for example, swords were intended for use against people in armor, and the design of the blade depended on the armor it was supposed to penetrate. Cutting through boiled leather is a lot easier than hacking through chain mail or plate.

By the way, the plate armor you think of when you hear the phrase "knight in shining armor" didn't come into use until the fourteenth or fifteenth century. That kind of heavy armor was invented because some bright boy came up with the crossbow. A crossbow bolt could punch right through the chain mail knights had been wearing, so they had to invent another way to protect themselves.

As the armor got heavier, the swords did too. A medieval sword is basically a club with edges. You battered at your opponent, breaking bones and doing as much damage as you could.

A knight fought with a sword in one hand and a shield in the other. He stood with the left side leading -- since the left hand held the shield -- and swung his right arm around to whack his opponent. I once saw a show on the History Channel that described knights as the tanks of the medieval battlefield -- all raw power and inertia that could roll right over an unarmored fighter.

But once guns came into wide use, plate armor

became useless. The musket balls of the time could punch through steel, so people quit wearing armor as agility became more important. However, swords were still more reliable than early firearms, which only fired one shot and took time to reload.

So during the Renaissance, swords became much lighter -- basically stabbing weapons rather than clubs. That resulted in a change of fighting style as the emphasis shifted to speed and skill more than the kind of brute strength a knight needed.

When civilians began to carry rapiers in the sixteenth century, innovative fighting techniques were developed that can be interesting as romance plot devices. Rapiers were light weapons designed for one hand, which left the other free for use in a variety of ways. A fencer could use a dagger or even a second sword in their left hand in what was called the Florentine style. The fighter could also carry a small round shield called a buckler -- that's where the expression "swashbuckler" comes from -- or wrap their cloak around a forearm to block or entangle an opponent's blade. Duelists were even known to carry lanterns during night duels, opening the shutter at strategic points to blind their opponents.

When you're writing a sword fight, do plenty of research specific to the period you're writing about. You may discover all kinds of nifty details that add interest and drama to your fight. As I've said before, it's the details that sell a story.

A great place to research this kind of fight is YouTube. Do a search on HEMA -- which stands for Historical European Martial Arts. HEMA reenactors try to recreate the techniques of medieval swordplay. Spend a couple of days watching HEMA videos and write down any moves that look like something you want to include in your fight.

You can research hand-to-hand the same way. One of my favorite channels for that is Fight Science (@fightscience), which explores hand-to-hand from a perspective of both criminal psychology and martial arts. The channel has a ton of videos, and it always gives me great ideas on things like how to spot an attacker before he strikes, or how to intimidate him into backing down. You'll also find tips on things like fighting multiple attackers. The presenter, Dr. Mark Phillips, breaks techniques down in a clear, understandable way I've used to make my fights sound realistic and believable.

If you're writing a cop, you'll also find great videos on how to do everything from handcuffing a resisting suspect to using a Taser.

Cops And Killers In Combat

Speaking of writing law enforcement characters, my husband is a cop. The following suggestions about writing police characters came from various discussions with him.

Writing characters in law enforcement is tricky. For one thing, there are something like 708,000 cops working for 18,000 agencies in the US, including police departments, county sheriff's offices, state troopers, and federal law enforcement. As if that wasn't complicated enough, each municipality, county, and state have their own laws and regulations, which can vary considerably from jurisdiction to jurisdiction. That makes research a necessity.

When it comes to fight scenes, if you're writing about a real-life law enforcement agency, you need to find out what specific kind of weaponry it uses. For example, the FBI used to carry Sig Sauers, but they've since switched to Glocks 19Ms, among others. Do your research! All this stuff is highly technical and easy to get wrong.

Cool Under Fire?

Then you need to think about how your protagonists handle being shot at. First, dodging bullets is basically impossible, since nobody but Clark Kent is faster than a speeding bullet. Us mere mortals must hide behind something, such as cars. An engine block makes pretty good cover -- nothing outside of an IED can punch through an engine block. Thus, cops like to put the front of their cars between them and the bad guys. Stone walls are also good.

On the other hand, bullets will punch right through doors or Sheetrock walls, so they don't make good cover at all.

Another factor you should keep in mind is how your protagonist does their job when under fire. Even if you're a skilled marksman on the firing range, being shot at is a whole different kettle of fish.

For one thing, when someone shoots at you, adrenaline floods your bloodstream. The blood leaves your cerebral cortex for your arms and legs so you can fight or run away. This is hell on fine motor control, which makes your hands shake. That, in turn, makes it harder to hit what you aim at. Training -- especially training under fire -- can compensate for this, but it's still a serious issue.

That's one reason cops are taught to aim "center mass" -- or at the torso -- of a subject. That's because the torso is a lot easier to hit than, say, the head, which is a relatively small target. Too, if you shoot somebody in the torso, chances are good you'll hit something that will make your suspect black out from lack of blood.

They even have a reasonable chance of living to trial if they get medical attention in time.

This, by the way, is why cops don't try to shoot the gun out of someone's hand. Only the Lone Ranger can pull off that trick. Ditto with shooting someone in the leg, which doesn't keep the guy from shooting back. Besides, it's entirely possible they'll die anyway, because if you hit the femoral artery, your suspect will bleed to death in minutes.

Police are also taught to shoot people armed with knives, baseball bats or other lethal weapons if they're close enough to use them. According to my husband, someone twenty-one feet away can run up and stab or club you before you can draw your weapon and shoot him.

Cops do *not* mess around with armed people.

However, you need to make it clear that your protagonist had no other choice than to open fire. Police can -- and should -- be charged if they use lethal force on someone who isn't really a threat.

Following a shooting, most police agencies put the officer involved on administrative leave while an investigation is conducted. If the situation is particularly egregious, they may get suspended.

Internal affairs will dissect everything the officer did and why they did it. All of which can make an interesting conflict for your cop protagonist as they wonder if they're headed to prison.

Gunfights

Every gunfight you've seen on film or television is largely bullshit

Despite what you've seen in movies and on television, people do not fly backward when you shoot them. They just fall down. Newton's Third Law tells us that a bullet that could send somebody flying when you shoot them would also send you flying in the opposite direction. So resist the urge to knock somebody through a plate glass window with a bullet.

Another hoary old favorite of bullshit TV is to have the character shot in the shoulder, which is supposed to be a "minor" injury.

Nope. There are many crucial bones, muscles, and tendons in the arms, assuming you don't bleed to death if the bullet hits an artery.

At the height of the crack epidemic during the 1990s, one of my husband's partners was sitting in his patrol car when a drug dealer walked up and shot through the door. The bullet hit his shoulder, and he ended up disabled, unable to use that arm. He was forced to retire, ended up addicted to prescription pain medication, and eventually died of a drug overdose. My husband and I were heartbroken; he'd been a damned good cop and a good friend.

Cops Never Surrender Their Weapons
Another myth: cops never give up their weapon to a hostage taker. Never. Nothing will make my husband scream obscenities at the television faster than some idiot cop hero throwing down his weapon because the bad guy has a gun to a hostage's head. Nuh-uh. All that does is get both cop and hostage shot.

The Art Of The KO
When you're writing a fight scene, you need to make the final blow dramatic and devastating. Again, YouTube is a great source of techniques for your character to use. And go for something unexpected. Never make the protagonists' victory easy or predictable.

This is especially true of the climax. After all, this is what you've been building up to for the past 400 pages. Make it both memorable and surprising. *Most of all, it must be something the protagonists do themselves.* You don't want two hundred cops coming to the rescue while the heroes sit in the car. That way lies anticlimax.

I read a book once in which the protagonists stood around watching while the two bad guys argued and finally shot each other. Uh, no. That was not a satisfying ending. Those bad guys had been doing evil stuff to the heroine all book long. I wanted her to get a little of her own back.

Your couple should administer the *coup de grâce* personally, just as they should pay dearly for their victory. They get shot, they get stabbed, they end up with broken bones and a hospital stint... though they're still in better shape than the villain, who should be headed to either jail or the morgue.

Anything less than that is too easy, and the reader won't enjoy it as much.

Chapter Eleven: Putting the Erotic in Erotic Romance

Obviously, if you're going to write erotic romance, your story must be erotic. But what does that mean, exactly, and how do you go about creating a sense of eroticism?

Eroticism isn't just sticking Tab A in Slot B. It's description -- the curve of his biceps, the way the light shimmers on the upper slopes of her breasts. The reader should feel the sexual tension start to build between the couple from their first glance.

What's more, *you* should feel it too, or you're in trouble. As many times as I've written love scenes, there are times I find it almost impossible to get a couple into bed. That's usually because I've been so focused on the conflicts that I've neglected to build sexual attraction. I have to go back and insert those elements until the passion begins to flow.

Linda Howard wrote a wonderful little checklist called "The Twelve Steps to Intimacy," which was based on the bestselling book *Intimate Behaviour* by zoologist Desmond Morris.

Because women are smaller and weaker than men, Morris says, the male partner must first build the woman's trust and cooperation before he can make love to her. He does this in a set sequence Morris says we all unconsciously follow.

In the initial stages, it's all about checking the potential partner out -- is he or she sexually attractive? That's why in almost every romance, no matter how "sweet," there's a moment in which the characters react to one another's looks.

I put this principle to use in *The Forever Kiss*, my

first novel. Vampire Cade McKinnon has gone to meet Valerie Chase at the airport. Cade has been sharing erotic dreams with Val for years, but this is the first time he's seen her in more than a decade...

Then he spotted a familiar, long-legged figure striding toward him. His throat tightened at the sweet symmetry of her face and the lush, tight curve of her breasts and hips.

Valerie.

She looked just as she always had in his dreams. Her face was a delicate oval set off by a pointed little chin and narrow nose, but her mouth was lush, with a hint of a wicked smile playing around its corners. (*Note: you want the description of your character to be individual, to create a strong mental impression in your reader's mind.*) She wore a summer weight cream suit that managed to look coolly professional even as it hugged her long legs. A silk blouse provided discreet coverage for round, pert breasts he knew from personal experience made a delightful handful. The blouse's mint green fabric contrasted against the dramatic tumble of auburn hair that frothed around her slim shoulders.

Valerie. There, in the flesh. Close enough to touch.

Cade's knees actually went weak.

Later, I described Val's reaction to Cade. But I also take the opportunity to ratchet up the conflict between the two when she recognizes him as Cowboy, the Texas Ranger who makes love to her in her dreams...

> "Ms. Chase, I'm Cade McKinnon," the man said, extending a big, gloved hand in greeting. His face was long and angular, with broad, jutting cheekbones, a deeply cleft chin, and a narrow nose. Despite those aggressively stern features, his mouth was intensely sensuous, with the kind of generous, mobile lips that could kiss and charm with equal skill.
>
> Val shook off her reaction to his sculpted male beauty and opened her mouth to attempt a professional greeting. Just as she met his eyes.
>
> Set just slightly aslant under black brows, their irises were a rich, dark chocolate. *God*, she thought, forgetting what she was about to say, *he's got the most beautiful eyes I've ever seen...* Entranced, she looked deeper.
>
> Suffering. Ruthless determination. And hunger -- devouring, threatening, somehow erotic.

She froze. It was Cowboy.

After the couple has that first eye-to-body contact, there's an electric moment when their eyes meet. Women will often instinctively drop their eyes or look away, since a direct stare is aggressive. Your Alpha hero, on the other hand, may hold the gaze until she meets his eyes again and gives him a slight smile.

That's his invitation to come over for the next stage: voice to voice, where the pair talk.

Next, Morris says, he may touch her hand, either by a handshake or in a simple brush of the fingers. After that, he'll touch her shoulders, then her waist. Anytime you make contact below the waist, it becomes overtly sexual, even if it's just a brush of fingertips along the knee.

Next comes the first kiss, which needs to be given a lot of attention. The kiss is a precursor to lovemaking, an indication of what we and the heroine can expect. How skillful is he? How tender? Build the anticipation.

The next step is a touch of the head. We've all seen couples play with each other's hair or caress faces. We all instinctively recognize this as intimate behavior.

It's at this point that the hero may touch her breasts. If your heroine's arousal doesn't match his, Morris writes, this is where she's going to call a halt. Much further along, and it's very difficult to get the male to stop.

Now we need privacy, because the next steps are mouth to breast, hand to genitals, and actual penetration.

According to Howard, if your hero skips steps -- going from talking straight to a kiss, for example -- that can be shocking and arousing, but he also runs the risk that the heroine will shut him down hard. Then he'll have to work to get back in her good graces again.

If you're having trouble getting your characters into bed, make sure you've laid the groundwork with these earlier steps. Once you build the attraction and passion between your couple, love scenes come much more easily.

Building The Romance Within Love Scenes

Do not treat your love scenes as porn breaks in the middle of the story. This is a problem I see even among published romance writers. They know their editors expect a love scene somewhere around Chapter Seven, so they just stick one in. The characters have a mechanical kind of sex that doesn't really reflect the development of their romance or who they are as people.

The rule I gave you for fight scenes -- escalate them to reflect the growing hate between your heroes and villain -- is also true of love scenes. Remember the first law of fiction writing: *show, don't tell.* There is no better way to show the love growing between your characters than the way they make love.

Since you're writing an erotic romance, the first encounter may be all about sexual attraction. Maybe they're making love for other reasons too: she's bartering for his protection, or they're blowing off steam from whatever dangerous situation they're in.

But the next time they make love, the reader should be able to tell a deeper emotional bond is beginning to develop. His touches are more tender. Her kisses are more intense. That intensity increases with every succeeding sexual encounter as they fall more and more in love. By the last sex scene of the book, their love is full-blown and intense, giving the encounter a sweetness that makes the reader's heart ache.

Love scenes can also reflect the romantic conflict. If the characters have just had a tearing argument, the scene should reflect that anger. Angry sex can be deliciously hot, as long as you avoid true brutality. Heroes don't hurt their heroines -- or vice versa.

Still, take every opportunity you find to build the romantic conflict between the characters, especially in scenes where you're working to heighten the eroticism. Doing both at once increases the tension for the reader.

Plotting Sex

As I've mentioned, erotic romance authors must often force the pace to get the characters into bed much sooner than normal. The trick, as always, is to motivate the scene by creating some external situation that requires them to sleep together. One possibility is the heroine's bartering for the hero's protection.

However, you need to set the situation up in such a way that he's the only one who can protect her. A writer who uses this device must also make sure to establish the hero has good reason to give the heroine this choice. Otherwise, we'll assume he's a jerk, and the heroine should blow him off and go hire somebody who isn't a lecherous pig.

In my novella "Blood and Kisses," in *Forever Kisses Vol. 2* the heroine offers the vampire hero her blood. Vampires in the twenty-third century are ostracized in that universe, so it's the first chance Jim Decker has had in decades to get laid. So he's got a good reason to accept.

For her part, my heroine, Beryl, is being hunted by a vampire assassin, and the only hope she has of protecting herself is another vampire. Again, she's motivated in a way the reader can understand and sympathize with.

What Would *You* Do?

In general, if it's something you wouldn't do, don't have your heroine do it. That's particularly true when it comes to bondage, one of my readers said in her answers to my survey.

"If I were a writer (and I'm not), I'd never write something with bondage between strangers," she wrote. "I can't help my pragmatic, somewhat streetwise side that screams, 'Are you fuckin' *nuts*?!' LMAO! In fact, there's only one guy I've *ever* known that I trusted enough for that."

Another reader agreed that the characters must have a reason to trust one another.

"I like them unpredictable, but safe," she wrote. "I need to be reasonably comfortable with the protagonists and the situation before sex occurs. There are exceptions, of course. The first erotic romance novel I ever read, Emma Holly's *Personal Assets*, has the heroine (of the A story) going down on the hero (of the A story) at the start of the first chapter. But by that time their relationship has already been established with considerable skill. Also, the situation is safe, it isn't a back alley somewhere, and the heroine, not the hero, is in control. That scene is also fundamentally *fun*. You can't put a price on that. If the characters are having fun, that just leaps off the page."

That last sentence is key. For erotic romance to work, the love scenes need to be fun. You can have angst coming out of your ears everywhere else in the book, but when those characters get into bed, they have a very good time. They may be angry with one another to start out with, but the sex needs to rapidly morph into something lighter.

If the sex is too emotionally heavy, it's not going to be erotic, just disturbing. An example of this is a novella I read by a very good erotic romance author. The hero was a partial eunuch and was unable to have an orgasm. The entire novella was about the hero's desperate struggle to get off. His orgasm was his and his heroine's sole focus. I did not find this story at all erotic, though I normally love this author's work. The characters were just working too damn hard to have any fun.

That's another reason to avoid characters with serious psychosexual issues, such as frigidity due to rape. The minute the sex becomes a form of therapy, you've lost about ninety percent of your heat.

On the other hand, you should mix the moods up a little, as one reader wrote. She said she liked love scenes that "involve doubts, fear, laughter, play, all the things that make us who we are. I love sex, a lot, but I won't spend every waking moment taking sex seriously, nor will I want to have it ALL the time. So, I really don't like seeing that in a story."

Variety is important, the readers agreed.

"I like reading scenes that surprise me," one wrote. "It can be through characterization, not just choreography/acrobatics. Missionary can still be interesting if the chemistry between the H/H is hot."

But don't forget the emotion, another reader cautioned.

"I like sex scenes where both parties (or all three) have an emotional connection. Where the reader feels, tastes, craves what the lovers have. The sex acts that occur because that is what the lovers like and want -- not because the writer decided to put something kinky in just because."

Making The Ordinary Sexy

Often, I look for a bit of business I need for plot purposes that might otherwise be a bit pedestrian, and I morph it into a love scene.

For example, in *Master of Wolves*, I had established that one of the first things werewolves learn is how *not* to infect someone with their bite. So I knew I had to have a scene where the hero gives the heroine a lesson in this. Now, being a vampire writer, any time you mention "bite," I think "sex." So the scene seemed tailor made for a love scene.

But I didn't want it to be a clichéd hero-teaches-heroine-to-make-pottery scene either, so I decided to throw in a little conflict while I was at it.

His fingers traced up her zipper, caught the tab, drew it down. Traced up again, over the silk and lace, drawing a line of heat up her belly. She gasped. "Jim!"

"Mmm?" He sounded lazily amused as he ran his thumb along the elastic band of her panties, slowly, as if considering dipping inside.

"Are we still practicing?" Her libido was definitely growling now.

"Practicing what?" His hand slid down her waistband. His palm felt deliciously warm. "Faith?" he prompted. "Practicing what?"

One finger stroked between her damp lips.

"Practicing… Oh!… Biting."

His fingertip circled her clit, almost touching it, but not quite. "Yes."

Pleasure spooled up her body in long, slick ribbons. "So we're not having sex?"

"Nope." The finger dipped into her slick core, then retreated again.

"Ummm. Feels like we're having sex."

He tugged her nipple through the fabric of her bra. "But we're not."

His cock felt like a steel rod against her ass. It was getting really hard to concentrate. She licked her dry lips. "So what are we doing again?"

He raked her clit with a teasing thumbnail. "Pissing you off." He jerked his hand from her shorts.

As she gasped in outrage, he presented his forearm to her teeth. "Bite."

Frustrated -- he was teasing her! -- Faith sank her teeth into the tangy masculine flesh. She felt the magic boil up, surging out of the Mageverse. Belatedly, she remembered the idea was to block it and tried to force it back down again. It refused to obey, surging through her jaws and into the impressions left by her teeth.

She opened her jaws and studied the bite in

dismay. "Shit. If you'd been human…"

"You'd have infected me." Jim released the breast he'd been toying with, grabbed her T-shirt, and whipped it off over her head. Before she could squawk a protest, he attacked her bra. A moment later, he dropped it on top of the shirt.

"So you're just going to torture me until I get it right?" she demanded.

"Basically." He nuzzled her ear and gave it a taunting nibble.

Eventually, I have *her* throw *him* down and bang his brains out.

You'll notice this entire scene is foreplay. The longer he teases her, the hotter the reader gets. There's a lot of built-in conflict in this kind of teasing, and it's also a good way for a character to establish dominance. Then you can have the other character turn the tables on him.

Dominance scenes have a lot of sizzle to them and many readers absolutely adore them.

"I love scenes in which a woman first gives up control of her orgasm to the man," one reader wrote. "That's a scary thing for me, letting go enough to trust that he'll take me over the edge. Whether it's aggressively done or sweetly, it doesn't matter. That type of scene gets me every time."

I did a lot of that kind of scene in *Jane's Warlord*, because Baran established his dominance every chance he got.

Baran had taken her before in calculation and in heat, but this desperation was new.

Jane could taste it in the way he kissed her, open-mouthed and fierce, his long fingers curling around the back of her skull, angling her head just the way he wanted it.

He took her in a long, sweet stroke of tongue and lip, hot and wet and hungry. Somewhere in the endless tumble into delight, she heard the rumble of a passing car, accompanied by the short, mocking toot of its horn. A tiny measure of sanity returned. Prying her mouth away from his, she panted, "We can't do this on the side of the road, Baran!"

"Yes, we can," he growled, and captured her mouth again, the kiss drugging, hungry. (*That's a bit of pure Alpha Male dominance there.*)

Jane wrestled free and threw a desperate glance around them, trying to determine if they were being watched. She realized she knew the area from her wild teenage years. "There's a spot down by the woods. A stream. We could…"

He looked down at her. The lust in his eyes was so intense, it didn't seem quite human -- and not just because of the fiery glow. His lips pulled back from his teeth in a slow, erotic smile. "Run. Before I take you on the hood of the truck." His powerful hands reluctantly relaxed their hold.

It wasn't an idle threat. Jane whirled and fled as if chased by something that would eat her. And with a little squirt of heat, she knew he intended to do just that.

She ran flat out, recklessly, plunging through the tangle of brush and trees, leaves crackling and flying around her booted feet. Throwing a glance over her shoulder, she saw Baran still standing by the truck, almost crouched, anticipation hot on his face. Even from yards away, she could see the erection tenting his jeans.

Then he exploded after her.

Jane sucked in a desperate breath, whipped her head back around, and ran for all she was worth.

Her heart banged in her chest as she ducked between a stand of trees and jumped a bramble bush. She could hear him gaining already.

God, he was fast.

Her nipples hardened as she imagined just what he'd do when he caught her.

The idea of being hunted by a big male predator is very erotic for a lot of women -- as long as both we and the heroine know he has no intention of hurting her.

By the way, one of the readers on my loop told a story about reading this scene out loud to her husband as they drove through the woods in a jeep. They both got so turned on, they stopped the jeep and enacted the scene!

Slow Hands

In general, I like to take my time with a love scene. Mine usually run between five and ten pages, because I want to make sure the readers are as turned on as the characters.

First, think about location. You don't always have to do it in bed. Actually, you may want to do it everywhere *but* bed, because other locations make the sex seem more spontaneous and exciting.

Create a sensual environment -- a garden in the spring, perhaps. The hero and heroine are sitting in the warm sunlight, listening to the lazy drone of bees and the chirp of robins. The air smells of roses and rich brown earth. He touches her...

Or maybe they're bathing together. I love writing love scenes in a shower or stream, because the water becomes almost a third partner in the sex. The shower spray beats gently on the skin, or the water caresses her as she swims through it. Think of sensory details: the smell and taste of rain. Is it cool lake water or a warm bubble bath? Build the sensuality before your couple even starts touching.

Next, think about who makes the first move. What kind of foreplay is he using? How does it feel? What position are they going to make love in? Remember: these people are going to be making love a lot, so it needs to be different every time.

Where are these characters in their journey to

love? What's their mood going into the scene? Are they angry? Frightened? Just plain horny? Use that. Express the emotion in the way they touch. Maybe he knows she's scared, so he's particularly tender with her.

When Jane and Baran first make love in *Jane's Warlord*, it's directly following a nightmare.

> He slid his hands up under the hem of her T, pushed it upward. She felt the cool draft on her erect nipples for only a moment before Baran's warm, long fingers covered one breast. Cupped lightly.
>
> *You don't know him,* sanity whispered.
>
> *I don't care.*
>
> His long hair tumbled across her skin as he lowered his head to find one nipple. The heat of his claiming mouth made her spine arch.
>
> "I've been wanting to do that for hours," he rumbled against her skin, and licked the pointed tip. "Ever since I scented your heat in that pretty red silk gown." He groaned. "God, that book of yours made you wet."
>
> She inhaled sharply. He gave her nipple a delicate rake with his teeth. Pleasure danced up her spine. "You... you could smell that? On my clothes?" She knew she should be outraged, but just now she was too grateful for the distraction.
>
> "Mmm," he said, and laughed, soft and

dark. "My nose is almost as good as Freika's. In fact, it tells me you're creaming now." He suckled, making her squirm.

"I can't believe you sniffed my nightgown..." She had to stop to gasp, "...when you'd never even met me."

That dark laugh rolled over her again, making her shiver. "I not only sniffed it, I seriously considered wrapping it around my cock." Another wicked almost-bite sent delight throbbing through her nipples as his long fingers squeezed and teased. "It's been a very long time since I've ridden a woman, and you tempt me."

Something about the rough, dark way he phrased it sent a quiver through her. "Yeah," she managed through the flood of heat, "I did pick up on that part. Your eyes glow whenever you're..."

"Aroused. Or angry." He swirled his tongue over one tight point, then lowered his head to find the curve where her rib cage met her waist. "You've got a talent for making me both."

He laved her bellybutton until she squirmed. Her giggle was cut off by his fingers hooking into the waistband of her sweats.

"I don't like these," he said. "Don't wear

them again." Before she could work up any outrage at that blunt order, he started pulling them down. "I want to feel your bare legs wrapped around my ass."

Her head spun. "Okay," she panted as he stripped them ruthlessly off. "But just so we're clear, you're not telling me what to wear."

Baran's eyes flashed at her through the darkness, red and bright as coals before he turned to toss the pants across the room. She heard the soft thump as they landed. "Oh, yes I am. You're going to do every last thing I order you to do."

"Not when you're just being a sexist jerk."

"Every last thing, Jane," he insisted, leaning close until his breath gusted warm on her ear. "Instantly. Without stopping to parse out whether you agree. Because it's the only way I can keep you alive." A big hand wrapped in the fragile fabric of her panties and twisted. The silk pulled at her hips and the tops of her thighs before it ripped.

"Hey!" She glared up at his dark shadow looming over her. "You didn't have to do that!"

His eyes gleamed as he moved back down her body like the erotic predator he was. "No, but I wanted to. Just like I want to do this." He dipped his tongue between her outer labia, a wet, tempting stroke along sensitive flesh and soft hair.

Again, I focused on description -- the way things feel, smell, and taste. I also kept building the conflict between them, with Baran giving those erotic orders of his, and Jane trying to refuse. This kind of dialogue always makes a scene hotter.

On the other hand, whenever you have one character dominate another like this, at some point you need to let the second character get a little payback.

In the last love scene in *Jane*, Baran submits to her, holding his arms still while she teases him. This is a big gesture of trust on his part, since I'd earlier established that Baran has a fear of being helpless stemming from a sexual assault.

It's very important to be as creative as possible with every sexual encounter, because you can bore readers easily. Many of my readers said they don't like long love scenes because they're so often badly done.

"There is only so much of 'he plunged his cock in her pussy' I wish to read," one wrote. "I'd say about 3 to 7 pages, and that is only if it's well written. Because, one page of badly written smut is just way too much for me."

Another reader said she's willing to read longer scenes as long as they're interesting.

"As long as it doesn't feel like a slow read, I really think it could be any length at all. I couldn't honestly say how long sex scenes usually are," she wrote. "That said, it should not be repetitive. Describe the hero driving the heroine to orgasm five times with his tongue and you will have lost me, no matter how wonderful I think it is that he would do that."

Everyone agreed boring a reader with sex is a fatal mistake.

"Anything much over three pages would probably have me tuning out and turning over the pages to get to the rest of the story, but I can't say I've really analyzed it, there have been a few books where I've basically gone, Oh God not another sex scene, and turned the page, no matter how short, then again someone like Morgan Hawke can have a prolonged scene going on for pages and my eyes will be glued to my book. Just don't put a sex scene in for the sake of adding another one, it shows. I've read some of the major publishers' 'erotic' lines that they've been bringing out, and probably in more than half of the books I've felt that I'd read more erotic scenes in a sweet romance, the authors/editors don't seem to have a feel for it, they're descriptive scenes but often cold and unemotional, not fitting easily into the flow of the book, and therefore unerotic."

How do you make sure you're writing hot?

The advice I always give is if you really want to turn on the reader, you must be turned on yourself. Don't try to write something that doesn't do it for you, because the reader will be able to tell.

If you're having trouble writing hot, I suggest trying a couple of twenty-page short stories which are basically nothing but the hottest sex scenes you can think of. Concentrate on the details and dialogue. It's dialogue that really stokes the sense of emotional involvement between the characters.

But keep any speech short and simple. As I've said before, if your characters are spouting reams of poetry, you're telling your readers they're not that aroused.

Another point: when you get to the penetration part of the program, don't make your hero too quick on the trigger. I remember reading some early romances where the hero came almost the moment he entered the heroine. Spin it out more. Make it clear the heroine goes away satisfied.

That's the best way to make sure your reader is too.

Pacing Love Scenes

No matter how hot your sex scenes are, avoid doing them back-to-back. I make sure I have plenty of conflict and action going on in between love scenes.

It's also very difficult not to be repetitive when you've got too many sex scenes one after another. You're better off with five deliciously hot love scenes than fifteen repetitious ones.

Another reason to space the scenes apart is that you need time to build the sexual tension. Make the reader turn pages faster and faster as she anticipates what delicious thing your heroic couple is going to try next.

Maybe they'll even get kinky.

Chapter Twelve: Erotic Romance and Kink

Mild kink has been a part of modern romance from the beginning. The first bodice ripper romances often included the heroine being tied up, and I remember several that featured spanking.

Gentle kink can even be found in mainstream romance. I once read a wonderfully hot scene in Christina Dodd's *My Fair Temptress*, in which the heroine ties the hero up and teases him while he threatens her with all kinds of delicious punishments.

That scene also demonstrates how delicately even mild bondage must be handled in these politically correct times. I was rather hoping he'd tie her up in return, but instead Dodd has him get his revenge in an opera box, where he teases the heroine unmercifully. She couldn't cry out for fear of being discovered -- psychological restraints instead of physical ones, mixed with a common fantasy: sex in public.

As I discussed in an earlier lesson, consent to whatever is going on is key, and both parties must enjoy the experience. What's more, you must establish that if the "dominant" in the scene thinks their partner does not consent, he or she will immediately stop.

Heroes and heroines do not commit rape, period. A protagonist's first concern is the well-being of their partner, not their own sexual pleasure. *Sexual abuse is not heroic.* The minute your hero commits rape, he's no longer heroic, and the odds are good the reader will sling your book across the room.

However, for some readers, it's not all that cut and dried. Sexuality and fantasy sometimes have nothing whatsoever to do with being politically correct, which is why e-pubs started exploring the concept of forcible seduction.

When No Means "Well, Okay…"

In this particular fantasy, the hero overcomes the heroine's reluctance to have sex by arousing her whether she likes it or not. There's a fine line between forcible seduction and rape -- actually, many people don't think there *is* a line -- and if you're not careful, you can turn readers off. In any case, if you write such a scenario, you can be pretty sure you're going to catch hell about it.

Yet some readers love the idea of being forced to have sex by a handsome stud, while enjoying every minute of it. For writers playing on that end of fantasy, having the submissive give verbal consent screws up the whole thing. Yet they still have to establish that the hero is not a rapist somehow. He cares about the heroine's physical and mental well-being, no matter what kind of games they happen to play.

One way to do this is by dipping into the hero's point of view. The heroine gives him plenty of cues that yes, she's turned on. What's more, he's willing to stop if she says *no* and means it.

When I first started writing erotica, I often did forcible seduction in short stories written for my own amusement. I grew up reading bodice rippers in the seventies, after all. Yet I'd always give the heroine a moment where she had the opportunity to stop everything by getting the drop on the hero. Instead, she chose to submit. I liked having the ultimate control in her hands.

Besides, if she just gets tied up and screwed without any say in it whatsoever, there's no internal conflict for her.

Unfortunately, even though this addressed consent from the heroine's point of view, it did nothing for the hero's. Sometimes I had him deliberately provide the heroine the opportunity to escape to make sure she consented. Even so, that's a little iffy, which is why I don't do forcible seductions today.

Heroes just don't do that kind of thing.

One writer who manages to pull forcible seductions off is Morgan Hawke, a good friend of mine. Her novel *Victorious Star* pushes the envelope just about as far as you can while still retaining sympathy for the heroes.

Morgan's primary hero, Ravanos, is a big, ruthless interstellar agent who kidnaps Imperial starship pilot Victoria Stark. The whole thing is part of a complicated plot to catch a traitorous starship captain.

Victoria, as an imperial officer, can't allow herself to be pressed into service for fear of losing her job. Ravanos and his first officer, Seht, give her no choice. The two men dominate her in a forcible seduction scene that pulls no punches at all.

It's not a book for those of delicate sensibilities -- it rocked me back on my heels more than once -- but Hawke manages to create sympathy for Ravanos and Seht in the complicated romantic triangle she constructs.

Actually, I'm not sure the book would have worked with just one hero, because at various times, Morgan creates sympathy by having one of them protect Victoria from the other. She also includes scenes of surprising tenderness as the men take care of their heroine, establishing they do care about her well-being.

Another factor in the book's success is that Victoria is nobody's victim. She's a true kick-ass heroine who is fully willing to go against anybody or anything for whatever cause she believes is right. At one point, in fact, she kills two men who were attempting to rape and murder her. So if she really wanted to, Victoria could find a way to kill Ravanos and Seht. She stays with them because she wants to.

I suspect that's one of the keys to making this kind of story work for a twenty-first century female audience. A hero can get away with a lot more when his heroine is a match for him in terms of strength, courage, and intelligence. If you tried to put an old-style timid romance heroine with a hero like that, he'd come off as a bully and a creep.

However, you still have to motivate the hell out of him. He's got to have a very good reason for whatever he does. His own sexual pleasure isn't enough; he must be serving a cause great enough to excuse what he does to the heroine. In Ravanos's case, he's trying to capture a mass murderer who will go on killing if he's not stopped.

Again, though, this kind of story is extremely difficult to pull off. I'd have multiple beta readers I really trusted if I was going to attempt it. Retaining sympathy in such cases is a delicate thing, often dependent on word choice and attitude.

It's much easier and less risky to have your characters play fully consensual sex games.

BDSM Play

As you might expect, Bondage and Domination/Sadomasochism, or BDSM, is a niche market that requires a delicate touch. *Victorious Star* is, in fact, a BDSM romance.

There is a whole real-life subculture built around "The Scene," as it's called, and I recommend that anybody planning to write about it do a great deal of research. One place to do it is https://fetlife.com/, an online community for the kinky. There may also be a BDSM community near you, depending on where you live.

In terms of sexual heat, the Scene can be a rich vein to mine, but again, you need to be careful in constructing your characters. You must give them good reason to get involved in BDSM. Then you need to explain to your probably vanilla readership what BDSM is, what the Scene is like, and what the rules are, in such a way that they won't decide your characters are perverts or dishrags.

Probably the touchiest part of writing a BDSM romance is establishing why your characters would want to get involved in bondage games to begin with. If you try to cast your hero as the kind of guy who just enjoys beating women, it's not going to fly. You must establish *why* your submissive is looking for somebody to dominate him or her.

From what I know of real-life Scene participants, subs are not the milquetoasts you see portrayed in popular media. Often, they're people whose day-to-day jobs involve their having authority over others -- such as cops, lawyers, doctors, or soldiers -- who feel a need to let someone else be in control for a while.

BDSM shares some characteristics with extreme sports: participants court danger for the adrenalin rush. Like marathon runners, submissives seek an endorphin high by pushing their bodies to the limit through pain and exertion -- and sometimes even fear. You can see why that's the sort of thing that would attract risk-takers.

In BDSM, being a sub is all about being the center of the game. The dominant's attention is totally focused on you and your reactions, even as he or she orders you around.

Dominants, on the other hand, have a more complex role. Their job is to provide that rush, often through the administration of physical or mental discipline. One of my critique partners, Diane Whiteside, writes about heroes who view the act of dominating someone as a gift to the submissive. Her vampire dominant Don Rafael can be deliciously ruthless with those who submit to him in books like *The Hunter's Prey* and *Blond of Blood*, but he always makes sure they enjoy the proceedings as much as he does.

The Dom has to take a great deal of responsibility for the sub's welfare and has to precisely judge what the sub needs and wants, even when the sub indicates otherwise. Sometimes submissives, high on endorphins, don't even realize they've reached their limits. When that happens, the dominant must call a halt.

Of course, that can be difficult, since the dominant isn't a mind reader -- unless you're writing paranormal. One way to make sure everybody is on the same page is to have your characters do what real-life BDSM participants do -- establish a safe word. Your sub can yell, "No! Don't! Stop!" all she likes, but if she uses a previously established safe word like "Rutabaga!" the Dom knows something is badly wrong and he's got to stop NOW.

Be Aware Of The Risks

That's a very good idea, since these games can carry real risks. Simply tying somebody up can be dangerous, if you leave them bound in the wrong position. Even police officers must be careful about the way they handcuff prisoners; people have been known to suffocate if bound with their arms so far back they can't breathe.

Never have a hero leave a bound person alone, and make sure he checks on the submissive frequently. They should never be left bound face down, and any gags should be carefully placed so as not to obstruct breathing.

As for more edgy play, such as whipping -- that's very tricky indeed. Be aware that if a dominant hits someone with a cane or whip across the back too hard, they can damage the kidneys and kill them. Strikes should be aimed at the backside, where there is a lot of muscle and padding and no internal organs to injure. I'd do some serious research on this before I attempted to portray any kind of physical discipline.

Practicalities

You should be equally careful when it comes to penetration, particularly anal. Your characters should use plenty of lubricant, or you'll provoke winces instead of arousal in your readers. Butter isn't a good choice -- it can cause infections -- and neither is spit, that favorite of the fictional rough trade. Petroleum jelly eats condoms, so that's out too. Something like KY is usually the lubricant of choice.

I once read a romance in which the villain loved to sodomize people using only their blood for lube. This is flatly unbelievable, as anyone knows who has ever had sex during her period. Blood isn't a lubricant. The minute it starts to dry, it turns into glue. Even though he cared nothing for his partner, the villain would have rubbed his own penis raw with that trick. So the bad guy would have used some kind of lubricant, if only for his own sake.

Remember, if it sounds as if it would be painful,

your reader is going to cringe and flip past the scene.

By the same token, never follow anal sex with vaginal sex. Your readers will know a nasty infection is sure to result, and infections just aren't sexy.

I recommend doing something like anal sex only after the characters have done a lot of careful, intense foreplay so that we know the sub is fully into it.

Most of all, *use condoms*. Period. I don't care if it is fantasy. If you're doing any kind of play in a contemporary setting, a character who doesn't use condoms is an idiot. Readers don't like stupid protagonists. In a paranormal, you can stretch that rule by explaining that your vampires or werewolves don't get sexually transmitted diseases, but if you're dealing with "regular" people, you've got to address the problem.

Radioactive Sex

You can get away with a lot, but there are some kinks that won't fly in erotic romance at all. Anything having to do with human waste or urine is out. You can't motivate that well enough no matter what you do.

Underage partners will also make a reader sling your book across the room, even if you're doing a historical set when people commonly married in their mid-teens. Readers don't want that much historical accuracy, thank you very much.

No dead people, with the possible exception of vampires. That includes zombies. There's nothing romantic about a partner who rots. Yeeeech.

As for bestiality -- no. An animal cannot consent. Of course, that gets tricky if you're doing werewolves. Frankly, I wouldn't have sex unless both partners are in human form, or they're both in werewolf form.

Again, AK's First Law is, "When they make love, everybody should have the same number of legs." If one of them is human and one four-legged, many readers will sling that book right into orbit.

Though not all will flinch. My friend Kate Douglas violates AK's Law of Legs regularly with her werewolf books, yet she manages to get away with it. If you're good enough, sometimes you can arouse your reader with an act that wouldn't normally appeal to her. I've had a couple of writers do that for me.

But in general, it's easier if you're not working in something that's too far out along the bell curve of sexual fetish. Particularly if it's painful -- such as whipping -- a good percentage of women aren't going to get into it. You should avoid playing in that particular kink if you're hoping for a big audience.

That said, the situation is different if you're writing for an audience looking for something they don't get from New York. In that case, you can get away with a lot more.

Which brings me to gay erotic romance.

Gay Erotica For Women

For many years now, one of the hottest sub-genres is gay erotic romance written for a female audience.

Men have always been fascinated by the idea of lesbians, probably because they like to fantasize about joining in. Yet women were assumed to want nothing to do with gay erotic romance. And, in fact, some women aren't interested in male/male romance at all. That may be because gay men in popular media have often portrayed as silly, effeminate stereotypes, played strictly for laughs.

Then romance readers discovered the world of

the hyper-masculine gay man, known in homosexual circles as the "leatherman." This is an Alpha Male with a taste for other Alpha Males, an idea women find exotic and fascinating.

A male artist friend of mine who went by the screen name ManofSteel posted the following vignette online. I thought it was so well done, I wrote and asked him if I could share it with you. Happily, he agreed. Even if you don't like gay stuff, I think you'll find this particular piece enlightening from the standpoint of pure craft, and as an insight into male sexuality.

To give you the setup: the star of MOS's stuff is David, who alternates between being the Dom and the sub in various people's fantasies. He's a bodybuilder, as is Brad, his rival/lover in this scene.

David's dialogue is pure Alpha Male. Watch the way MOS handles characterization. He says a lot about these two guys in 1,300 words. This story also has a beginning, middle, and an end, as well as a conflict that is perfect for its short length.

If you write gay erotica, you should also pay attention to the way MOS handles sex. It's rougher and more earthy than what women do, which is something you need to keep in mind when writing m/m. Men generally tend to play harder with each other than a man would with a female partner.

* * *

His voice was gruff. "Come on Brad! I don't suck just anybody's dick!" He leaned back so that my face was buried in his ass crack. "Work for it!" And I did.

His ass was a thing of beauty, a true bubble butt of pure grade A muscle. Watching him in the gym was mesmerizing. He usually wore those thin, tight, stretchy little hot pants that barely covered his ass, or he'd wear a leotard or tights, whatever you want to call them. All I know is that they looked like they were painted on. They were tissue thin, but totally opaque, and that was his "out." He wasn't showing off because you couldn't see through them. As if you needed to! I think that just made it worse! He didn't wear a jock. You would have been able to see the straps. There was just that thin, thin fabric… a film of threads that separated the actual view of his flesh from your eyes, but every curve of the huge beast between his legs was there for you to see, and when he'd bend down or squat, and then stand, he'd inevitably have to "adjust himself" down there, grab that monster, pull his balls out from between his crushing thighs to let them hang free and forward.

Sometimes I'd work the juice bar, and I'd see him slowly striding toward me, and two things would happen instantly: I'd get hard, and I'd get nervous. Now, I don't mind getting hard in public, but I don't like getting nervous. I want to be the one to make people nervous, and when he'd come over I felt like one of those schoolgirls that giggles and wants to feel my biceps, because I wanted to feel his biceps. I wanted to grab his fucking ass! I wanted to twist his nipples and bring him to his knees and reduce him to a pile of spurting moans.

But that's how he made me feel, without even trying.

He's six foot six. So you gotta understand that when he comes up and leans against a countertop, his cock and balls are right at the level of the counter. I mean, right on the edge. So naturally, it's uncomfortable to have an edge pressing against your parts, so whenever he'd come up to the counter, he'd have this shit-eating grin on his face, because he knew that I knew what he was gonna do, and sure enough, he'd do it. He'd lean up against the counter and then he'd kind of back away an inch, tilt his hips up, and rest the whole couple of pounds of sex meat and balls on top of the counter, and all the while he'd have this smirk on his face, like he didn't know what he was doing, as though it was inadvertent, unavoidable, not his fault, as though there was nothing he could do about it.

It was maddening. Because, like, you weren't supposed to stare. You weren't supposed to notice, but there was that package, that pole and those nuts, jutting out, barely clothed. He knew what he was doing. I tried to act like I didn't care, but he knew I wanted him. He just had a way about him.

He'd lean forward, and those pecs would practically spill out of his tank top. He'd drill his eyes into you. You simply cannot take that stare for more than a few seconds, and he knew it. He'd scratch his chest, He'd scratch his head, just to make his biceps bulge, and he'd watch you trying not to notice. Any way he moved was pure, animal, strip-you-of-every-inhibition, I-know-you-want-me, let's-do-it-right-here-right-now sex. Even when I asked him what size drink he'd want, he'd pause until I turned around, and then he'd flash that predatory grin, and say: "...large..."

And he made that one word just reduce me to a dripping, throbbing, trembling fool. And then, once he had his drink, he'd turn around, take a few steps, and stop. And he'd stand, as though surveying his domain, legs spread, hips tilted, so that one globe of muscle was slightly higher than the other, and then, in a move that made me want to bang my head against the wall, he'd slowly shift his weight to the other foot, and those meaty spheres would rise and fall, and I'd feel like I was losing control, like I was gonna leap over that counter, grab the waistband of his tights, and in one huge movement rip them all the way down to his knees and shove my cock up his ass and rape him right there in front of everybody.

I wanted that ass!!! I wanted it. I wanted it so bad.

And now, in my dream, I had it. But it was all wrong. I wanted to be the top. I wanted to hear him plead. I wanted to make him spurt with my touch when and where I wanted him to. But I buried my face in his ass and I licked his quivering hole so that he'd suck my cock. I was held prisoner by those thighs. His balls rested beneath my chin, and they were hot. His huge, slick, fuck rod sat in the groove between my pecs, and when I did a good job, he'd rock his hips and he'd fuck my chest. And if I was really good to his ass, he'd scoot back for a minute, bend down, and go down on me.

"That feel good, Brad?" he said.

I moaned. I was in ecstasy. He shifted his hips from left to right and rubbed his cock on my face. I moaned. My mouth was open, hungry. I tried to lick it. I wanted it again so bad. And in the meantime, my cock was being sucked by that handsome face, and he was good. He was sloppy and slow, just how I like it. He would do these things that made my eyes fly open. He'd roll his tongue around and around the head of my cock until I was on fire, and then he'd lick the staff, not enough to make me cum, but enough to make me want to so bad, and I'd lose control and start jabbing the air.

"Please Dave! Oh God! Please make me cum!"

He'd squeeze me with his thighs, and oh God that was a turn on. He scooted forward, and suddenly I was desperate for that cock on my face again. I whimpered.

"You want to cum, Brad?"

"Oh God! Oh God! Dave!"

"Work for it."

I dove into his ass again. I hated the fucker for making me a slave, but I just kept telling myself that this tight, little hole I was licking, was my ticket to making him cum again, to making him shudder and explode, and in that moment I'd throw him off me, spread his legs, and sink my throbbing cock into my prize.

With my tongue, I swirled and probed. I jabbed wetly between his leg and ball sac and wiggled my tongue.

"Damn, baby! Ohh!" He jerked. His grip on my thighs tightened. He started panting for breath. "God DAMN that feels good!" His whole body turned rock solid, and he started to tremble, and then his voice lowered and there was a desperate, "Oh!" So I licked faster. I tried to bite the flesh between his balls and hole and managed to get a good grip on it with my teeth and I very gently nibbled.

"OHHHH!!!!!" He nearly collapsed on top of me. He regained his posture and then the hips started rocking. I could feel the heat of his meat on my chest. He started rocking faster and whimpering. I wiggled my face back and forth to get in deep and I nibbled all around his hole.

"OHHHH!!! Fuck!" He nearly jumped out of his skin, and then he really started to rub his cock between my pecs.

"B-Brad? Oh geez! Brad...I'm gonna..."

"Yeah!" I yelled. I had him. He was mine I'm gonna make the fucker cum! Make him cum!

"...h-hot load of fuck cream all... all over your chest!"

"Give it to me!" I clutched his buttocks and drilled my tongue tip into his hole.

"Oh God! OHHH!!"

* * *

Obviously, this story is not a romance of any kind -- it's a sexual contest between two men, which Brad ends up winning. A recurring theme in MOS's stuff is the submissive who turns the table on the physically superior dominant by means of sexual skill.

This scene also has a definite story arc. He hooks

you in the first line, establishing David as the dominant: "I don't suck just anybody's dick. Work for it."

Then MOS shifts into a flashback to set up the conflict. He establishes David as both a tease and a physically intimidating presence that radiates Alpha Male sexuality. "Any way he moved was pure, animal, strip-you-of-every-inhibition,   I-know-you-want-me, let's-do-it-right-here-right-now sex. Even when I asked him what size drink he'd want, he'd pause until I turned around, and then he'd flash that predatory grin, and say:… large…"

He also gives you a sense of Brad, without ever describing him in an overt way. "Now, I don't mind getting hard in public, but I don't like getting nervous. I want to be the one to make people nervous, and when he'd come over I felt like one of those schoolgirls who giggles and wants to feel my biceps, because I wanted to feel his biceps." Again, there's a strong sense of character there. Not particularly admirable character, maybe, but very strong anyway. The lust you expect, but not the nervousness.

In the sex scene itself, you don't get the tenderness that you get with m/f sex, but there is a lot of raw heat.

MOS also does a good job of capturing speech. You feel as if Brad is telling you the story, thanks to his informal language, run-on sentences and repetition. *I wanted that ass!!! I wanted it. I wanted it so bad.*

MOS also uses my favorite trick of having David issue orders to his lover. One of the hallmarks of an Alpha Male is that they're leaders, and leaders give orders -- even in bed.

"You want to cum, Brad?"
"Oh God! Oh God! Dave!"

"Work for it."

Note the short sentences. Again, MOS communicates heat and dominance. Then he brings both David and the story to a climax when Brad makes him come, thus winning the sexual competition between the two.

Now, of course -- we're not writing gay erotica for gay men. We're writing gay erotic romance for straight women. There does need to be tenderness and love between the protagonists.

Morgan Hawke does a great job striking that balance in gay romances like *Tempestuous*. Both her heroes are definitely men, and they act like it, but there's also a beauty and tenderness to the couple's love that any fan of sweet romance would recognize.

And that's what readers are really looking for, regardless of the number of penises involved.

Section Five -- Craft
Dialogue and Prose that Sings

Chapter Thirteen: Silver-Tongued Devils

There's no better place to show characterization than in dialogue. Yes, actions speak louder than words, but in fiction -- which is all words anyway -- it's dialogue that adds life and sparkle.

By the same token, flat, stilted dialogue will kill a story no matter how well-plotted it is. So you need to pay particular attention to what's coming out of your characters' mouths.

Remember that we writers are essentially actors in our own heads. You're your hero, your heroine, and your villain, as well as the guy who delivers the pizza. And like a fifties method actor, you need to ask yourself, "What's my motivation?" every time you start a scene.

Hopefully you've done a GMC chart for all your major characters, so you should know what the characters' motivations are. But you also must communicate those goals and motivations as you write your dialogue. Remember: it doesn't count if it's not on the page.

As you play out those GMCs, don't forget that conflict is the bread and butter of drama. When it comes to your protagonist couple, most of their conflict takes place in dialogue. Here's an example from "Galahad," in the *Bite* anthology.

> "Ninety percent of what you've heard about me is bullshit," Galahad told her.
>
> "Yeah? My trainer said you Round Table guys are stone killers who go through women like toilet paper." *Keep your distance,*

Sir Fangsalot.

He stuck the cigar between his fangs and grinned around it. "You got me on the first part. Not sure about the second." Puffing, he allowed an artistic pause to develop. "I've never used toilet paper. Last time I took a dump, Europe was sliding into the Dark Ages." Before she could think of a suitable response to that one, he flicked his cigar into the ashtray. "So what brings you to the Lords' Club, Caroline? You do realize the Ladies' Club is across the street, right?"

Apparently Sir Galahad was a sexist jerk. That made things a lot easier. "I guess you didn't get the memo. Men and women are equal now."

He gave her a long look that somehow made her feel like a bitch. "Maybe, but witches are better than everybody. Which is why there are two clubs. All that blood and sex is so distasteful."

And maybe she needed to quit being so defensive before she alienated the only guy who could help her. "That's what I get for making assumptions."

"I forgive you." He stretched out his long legs, mailed heels clanking on the hardwood floor as he studied her. "Mostly because of those shorts. Is that fabric, or just layer of magical spray paint?"

Caroline glanced down. She wore the same snug denim cutoffs and cropped T-shirt she'd had on when she sat down to watch TV. "I forgot I was wearing these. I came right over when I had the vision."

"Yeah, I figured I didn't owe this little encounter to good karma." He rolled out of his chair with a boneless grace that suggested he wasn't kidding about the enchanted armor. Caroline followed as he sauntered over to the bar and pulled a glass down from an overhead rack. "I assume this vision did not involve you, me, and a pair of fur-lined handcuffs."

Readers love this kind of snarky dialogue. And it's a lot of fun to write too.

The key to pulling this kind of thing off is word choice. A character's sex, economic class, education, job, and moral background all influence how they speak. We wouldn't expect a fundamentalist preacher to swear like a sailor, nor would we expect a homeless bum to use six syllable words -- unless we first establish he was a college professor before he lost everything.

However, that doesn't mean you can't play against type. We wouldn't expect gallant Sir Galahad to say something like, "The last time I took a dump, Europe was sliding into the Dark Ages." Readers instantly want to know more about this guy.

I'm going to pick out a couple of sentences from some of my stories and let you see if you can guess what kind of character said them.

A. "I need you over at the hotel. Looks like somebody set off a bomb. And we've got bodies. At least twelve."

B. "Magic will not work in this room. Not yours, not mine, and not our fool of a sire's."

C. "You have committed fratricide, Llyr Galatyn. Under the terms of your father's will, you are no longer fit to rule."

D. "I'm going to do whatever it takes to catch Druas and keep you alive. So don't push me. You won't like the results."

E. "Look, you guys don't know this time, and you don't know this culture. You need my help, and that means I have to know as much as I can about that sick bastard."

A. A cop. Generally cops tend to use shorter, tighter sentences, though they also throw in longer jargon phrases, particularly when they're talking to superiors. They're also big on sentence fragments and leaving out words. You need to have a good knowledge of what kind of jargon those with a particular job will use.

B. The villain, who is a Sidhe king. The cadences and word choice might lead you to think the story is a historical, but in this case, it's a contemporary. I used words like "sire" and a more formal sentence structure to communicate the idea of royalty. Note the repetition of "not." Generally, it's better to avoid repetition, but it's fine when used for emphasis.

C. A Sidhe noble, talking to a king. Note the longer words and sentences designed to communicate the idea of great formality and seriousness. The lack of contractions heightens the formality.

D. The hero. Again, short, punchy sentences. He's telling you what he's going to do, not asking permission. Alpha males never ask permission if they can help it. You can like it or lump it.

E. The heroine, arguing with the hero. Again, I used repetition for emphasis. "You don't know this time, and you don't know this culture." In contrast to the hero's blunt speech, she's trying to reason with him, giving him a list of arguments for what she wants to do.

You'll notice I keep the speeches relatively short, even when I'm writing a character from the nobility. My rule of thumb is I rarely let my characters talk for longer than two manuscript lines without having someone else break in. Sometimes you need more, of course, but if I can tighten it, I do. Keeping dialogue short gives a sense of wit and movement.

I learned this during a stint writing comic books early in my career. I used to be long-winded, but there's not much room in a comic book for reams of dialogue. I quickly found I had to cut the heck out of my lines.

Then I noticed my comic book dialogue sounded much stronger than the stuff in my novels, because the shorter lines had more impact. Now I make a point of going through every sentence and cutting anything redundant.

Getting The Last Word

The last word of a sentence is where the most impact falls. Be careful not to blunt its impact.

"I'm going to hit you with a hammer sooner or later," has much less impact than, "Sooner or later, I'm going to hit you with a hammer." In the first example, the emphasis was on "later." In the second, it's on "hammer." Which is a hell of a lot more threatening.

Actually, I'd probably kill the phrase "sooner or later" altogether. "I'm going to hit you with a hammer," is a blunt, tight threat.

Kill all those little vampire phrases that suck away a line's impact. That includes calling a character's name at the end of a sentence. "I'm going to kick your ass, Joe," has less punch than, "Joe, I'm going to kick your ass." Again, you want the emphasis on the threat, not on the character's name.

Give every sentence a long, hard look. If its construction seems awkward or complicated, see if you can simplify it by cutting and rephrasing. You want your writing as clean and clear as you can make it.

The Soul Of Wit

I also love ping-pong dialogue, where characters are volleying lines back and forth. Here's an exchange from *Jane's Warlord* between my futuristic hero, Baran,

Passionate Ink   Angela Knight's Guide to Writing Romance

and his talking wolf, Freika. They've broken into the heroine's home, planning to install themselves as her protectors. But then Freika discovers Jane's cat...

> "Baran, it's under the bed," the wolf called from upstairs. "I see its eyes glowing."
>
> "Leave it alone, Freika." He turned the faucet off with a snap of his wrist.
>
> "But I'm hungry!" A snarling feline yowl rose. "And do you hear the way it's talking to me?"
>
> "Eating the target's cat would not create the first impression we want."
>
> "Just one bite?"
>
> "No. This is going to be difficult enough as it is without you snacking on her furry friends."
>
> "How could anybody be friends with a *cat*?"
>
> "Well, for one thing," Baran said, walking into the living area, "it's soft, it purrs, and unlike some I could name, it doesn't mouth off."

I often like to take a phrase and twist it just enough to give it a touch of humor, which is how I ended up with "snacking on her furry friends." Sometimes I look at a line and think, "You know, that

- 174 -

could be funny…" Then I play with it until I come up with a way to make it sparkle.

By the way, the cat bit ended up being a running joke all through the book. Judging by the comments I got, the readers loved it.

Dialogue Tags

Dialogue tags serve a useful purpose, since they let us know who's speaking and avoid reader confusion. At the same time, though, you want to use tags with a light hand, because they tend to break up the flow of the dialogue.

As in the previous scene, it's a good idea to leave off the tags whenever you can. You don't need "said" or "explained" when it's clear from the action who's talking.

Also, avoid weird tags. "He expostulated" is the mark of an amateur. If you're going to use a tag, "said" is generally your best bet, unless the way the character says the sentence is important. "Fire!" he bellowed.

It's better to give the character something to do and let that action be your tag. "Leave it alone, Freika." He turned the faucet off with a snap of his wrist.

Remember the magic words: *simplify and cut*.

Words Of Love

Dialogue is vital during love scenes because you can use it to establish the emotional connection between the characters. I once got a comment from an editor in which she said the heroine seemed "detached" from what was going on in a love scene. I added a little dialogue, and that took care of the problem.

Besides, readers love dialogue during sex.

"They shouldn't fall suddenly silent the second

their hands touch," one of my readers wrote in her response to my questionnaire. "I like some dialogue during, especially since it's often the most intense, compact way to communicate where the characters are at. 'Oh, God, harder!' is always going to be hotter than 'as if he could read her mind, the heroic George began to thrust harder...' Ridiculous illustration, I know."

You can even get away with a little bit of humor in your love scenes, another suggested.

"I haven't read it often, but occasionally a sex scene contains a joke or two. That can be really cool. I'm a sucker for those occasions -- rare in fiction, though not in life! -- when someone accidentally elbows someone, or knocks over a glass of water on the nightstand while reaching for a condom. I'd like to know that the characters I'm reading about could handle the odd bedroom mishap with smiles on their faces. I'd like to know that the hero could cope if the heroine burst out laughing while acting out his long-cherished dominatrix fantasy."

As I've said before, remember that the hotter you are, the less inclined you are to talk.

"Obviously they should not be holding entire conversations during sex or even during foreplay; one would hope their minds are on other things. All references to previous lovers should be absent, too, although the men I've known haven't always viewed this point the same way."

"I've never been able to keep a conversation going at something like an intellectual level once we get really going," another agreed. "A few short words concerning the situation, but that's about it. Best time for conversation is the afterglow."

Another reader agreed the dialogue doesn't have to be terribly coherent.

"In the bedroom, partners have to know how to make each other feel great. Otherwise, it's boring. To be blunt. LOL. Speaking is a great way to do that. Moans, whimpers, those work as well. If a couple doesn't speak when they have sex, it shows distrust in each other. You have to trust that your partner will enjoy your murmurs, not laugh at them. Most of the time, if there's no speaking, it's because the H or the h don't want to be there. Which means, the scene fails in my mind. That being said, there are exceptions. Danger, proving a point, etc. These things are plot situations that force the H and h to act differently."

However, the subject of conversation should definitely be each other.

"Not saying discussing the fact the car doors were not locked during sex is a good thing, but if they are confident enough to say what they like, and when they need it, or how the other one feels or tastes... *insert fireworks here*. Some dialogue can be extremely hot."

Too, dialogue is a great way for the hero to establish his sexual dominance in those luscious Alpha games readers love.

"Mmmm. You're slick."

A thick finger slid inside, tore a gasp from her mouth. "Oh, God, Baran, you make me..."

He grinned darkly. "I noticed. You liked being chased, didn't you?" With his free hand, he pinched and rolled her nipple. "Didn't you?"

"Yeah. Oh, yeah." She whimpered softly.

His glowing eyes narrowed as he studied her with predatory calculation. "You do realize I can do anything I want to you?" The question was asked in a velvet purr that would have made her wet even without the stroke and slip of those possessive fingers. "You're totally helpless."

Jane swallowed at the jolt of desire that sliced through her at the dark promise in those words. "Not totally," she managed, as feminist instincts rebelled.

"Totally." It was a soft growl. The hand tormenting her sex slid away. She looked down just in time to see him reach into a jeans pocket and pull out a familiar length of gold cable. "Or you're about to be."

"Oh, no you don't!" Jane started to sit up.

"Oh, yes," he purred, "I do." Before she managed more than an outraged yelp, he grabbed her shoulder and flipped her over on her belly. She tried to push up, run, but he slung a leg over her butt to pin her. Grabbing one wrist, he whipped the cable around it.

She gasped as he captured her other hand and pulled it down to join her captured wrist, then looped it in cable. The cool, slick metal tightened its grip, binding her hands at the small of her back. As her spine arched helplessly with her position, dried leaves teased her erect nipples. "You big jerk!"

"The operative word there is 'big'," Baran said, a dark chuckle in his voice. He grabbed the waistband of her jeans and jerked downward. Cool air flowed over her backside as he bared her. "And getting bigger by the second."

Again, don't be afraid to have your Alpha Male character push it with his dialogue, asking the heroine questions about her arousal and gently forcing her to answer. That adds another layer of heat to the scene.

Less Is More

Understatement can be your friend too, especially when you're writing villains. It's hard to take a bad guy seriously when he sounds like something out of a comic book.

In this scene, Ridgemont is torturing the hero, Cade, during combat…

Ridgemont grabbed his shoulder, easily holding him off the ground. Slowly, deliberately, the vampire twisted the blade. Cade dropped his sword and shield to clutch futilely at his torturer's wrist. Blood bubbled between his lips. His face paled as he visibly fought not to scream.

"Your guard dropped a bit at the end," Ridgemont told him, his tone as cool and clinical as a surgeon's. He dipped the blade to let his victim's feet touch the ground again. Panting in agony, Cade met his gaze with a hot glare.

Ridgemont grinned, planted a foot against Cade's crotch, and kicked him off the sword. Staggering, he fell hard with a wheezing gasp of pain.

His sire lifted the gory sword as if to behead him. Panting and unarmed, Cade curled his bloody lips in a sneer. The sword arced down. Val screamed.

The point buried itself in the sawdust an inch from his throat.

"I do hope you'll give me a better fight than this when the time comes, gunslinger," Ridgemont taunted. "Otherwise it will be somewhat… anticlimactic after one hundred and twenty years." The master vampire turned and swaggered away. "All right, Hirsch, it's your turn…"

Think about contrast when you're writing -- a violent act paired with a seemingly mild line of dialogue: *Your guard dropped a bit at the end.* This makes the character seem even more cold and threatening. Vicious cruelty isn't a big thing to him.

Don't be afraid to let your hero's nasty side show either. In this scene from *Forever Kiss*, Ridgemont is attempting to use his powers to force Cade into joining in on his assault on Cade's then-lover, Caroline. Cade deliberately goads him so Caroline can escape.

The ancient laughed and cupped her breasts in both hands. "You may as well stop fighting it, McKinnon. You just don't have the power to keep my mind from overriding yours." Lazily he tugged her nipples. "She's got pretty tits, doesn't she? So full and white." Ridgemont lowered his head and said into her ear, "Think of it, Caroline. Two cocks, two sets of fangs. It's going to hurt -- and I'm going to make you like it."

The widow's gaze flew to Cade's and silently begged. His expression hardened with determination even as he slid his jeans down his long, muscled legs. "Did *you* like it, Ridgemont?"

"Like what?" the ancient asked as he squeezed and fondled Caroline's breasts.

His voice was low and deadly. "Did you like it when the Saracens took their turn on you, back when you were mortal?"

Ridgemont's big hands stilled, his mouth going slack with shock.

"While you were so busy invading my

mind during the Change, I got a look at yours." Naked, Cade stepped up to him and looked down into his eyes with a taunting smile. "Your precious Lionheart hesitated too long about ransoming you when you were captured by the Saracens during that Crusade. And they got a little bored. It's been eight hundred years, but no matter how many women you rape, you can't forget what it was like being on the other end of the cock."

The ancient shoved Caroline aside with a roar of raw fury. She fell, then scrambled to her feet and lunged for her clothes, not even glancing around as Ridgemont strode across the room and drove his fist into Cade's face. He crashed into the wall, but she didn't look back as she balled up her things and ran naked out the door.

… As Cade went reeling from another pile-driver punch, Ridgemont drew up short, visibly working to bring himself back under control.

Licking the blood from his split lip, Cade stood, though he had to brace his back against the wall to do it. He grinned viciously, a demonic light in his dark eyes. "Oh, come on, Eddie -- be honest with yourself. You liked it all those centuries ago. In fact, you don't really want me to fuck Caroline -- you want me to fuck *you*."

Ridgemont, being a homophobe, promptly kicks Cade's ass. As Cade intends, this gives Caroline a chance to escape.

Don't pull your punches at times of high emotion, even if it means having a hero say something completely shocking. Shock is better than boredom any day.

Which brings me to language.

F-words and C-words

One of the questions erotic romance writers often wrestle with is what to call various body parts and sexual activities. Should you go with a euphemism, or fall back on four-letter words?

Now, some older readers take great offense to words like "fuck," "cock," "cunt," etc. However, they're usually not the ones reading erotic romance. Personally, I've always used whatever juicy Anglo-Saxon expression fit the moment.

My Red Sage publisher briefly outlawed "fuck" years ago because someone called and read her the riot act over its use. Now, I'd been using "fuck" in my Red Sage stories for years, and I was surprised when my editor suddenly made me take them all out. I did manage to work around the ban without falling back on euphemisms. That made me wonder if I used the word too often, which isn't good either.

At the other end of the spectrum, Changeling Press publisher Margaret Riley has outlawed euphemisms. She believes that using vague words like "core" for vagina or "rod," for penis is downright ridiculous. We write erotic romance, and millennial and Gen Z readers like their love scenes hot, sexy and a little raunchy. Vague words lack erotic power and energy, and often sound a little ridiculous. I'm thinking specifically of the cringe-inducing "manhood" found in old bodice rippers.

For similar reasons, I'd steer away from medical terms like "penis" and "vagina." They tend to sound cold and not at all sexy.

One of my author friends joked that we should use terms like "yoni," which is a Hindu word for female genitalia, or just make up our own sexual vocabulary. I might do that if I were worldbuilding a futuristic or fantasy setting.

My readers, as usual, also had strong opinions on the subject.

"'Fuck' is a great word," one wrote. "As a verb, it fills a hole in the English language. I'll take 'fuck' over 'make love' in most situations. It usually doesn't ring true for me to have a male character say he wants to 'make love' to the heroine, for instance, especially at a point in the story where he quite patently doesn't love her. And if she cries, 'Do it to me!' I will probably shut the book."

"C's and F are clear enough for me. I even like using them myself to shock people periodically. It kinda pulls you out of the scene if 1. the euphemisms are funny or 2. you don't understand what exactly is happening -- like a game of Twister."

That said, however, you can overdo the use of "fuck," another reader pointed out.

"Recently read a book by a new author that would have been a good read except that she put in C's and F's in all the sex scenes, and it was totally unbelievable on the part of the characters. It was as though she felt that using those words automatically made the scenes more erotic/hotter. I'd have liked to get my hands on the editor and asked them what they were thinking of. They do tend to strike me as odd in anything that's got an alien protagonist, why not make up a word, the reader should be able to tell from the context. I don't mind pussy, dislike dick and (I've seen this one a few times) totally hate kitty. A mature woman talking about her kitty is just wrong, it's juvenile enough to make me start thinking pedophile. Yuck. As a one-off joke, it's acceptable but other than that a thousand times no."

Morgan Hawke once made the observation that men use "cock" when they're getting ready to put the organ in question *into* somebody, and "dick" when they're just talking about it in general. "Penis," on the other hand, is a word they only use when talking to a doctor.

Readers agreed.

"I prefer cock over penis any day. Dick will do... Clit is essential, I think, if he's going down on her."

Writers should also be aware of our friends over the pond, as a reader from England pointed out.

"The only other word I can think of that needs to be used with extreme caution is 'fanny,' which, as most authors will probably be aware, means something rather different in the US from what it means to the rest of us. (As a teenager I was VERY confused by the lyrics to the theme tune of _The Nanny_. Ouch)"

In the United Kingdom, "fanny" is a slang expression meaning "vagina."

Note that there's some disagreement between readers here. When it comes right down to it, use your best judgment and do what works best for your story.

By the way, in the original edition of this book, this chapter was far longer as I explained what words readers did and didn't like.

In the almost two decades since, two whole generations of readers have come on the scene, and I wondered whether those guidelines still applied. I cut about sixty percent of the chapter, then asked my fellow writers if they knew how Gen Z felt on the subject.

Jessica Coulter Smith consulted her Gen Z daughter, who said they had no problem with the cock, cunt, pussy and fuck, but there are certain words and actions that will make her age group drop a book. They are:

Panties, mewling, plunged (ooops. I use that one a lot.), baby as a pet name, pecker, and putting a finger to the heroine's lips to shush her. Some of those I could see, since they're kind of sexist, but...

"What, they don't wear panties anymore?" I meant the question honestly.

"I think they just call them underwear."

I'm also told "moist" and "sopping wet" are bad. (I'd agree on sopping wet. Also dripping and leaking. Mostly because women don't actually drip, no matter how aroused they get.)

The thing about writing romance since dinosaurs roamed the earth is the rules change on you. My way of dealing with this problem is to follow Gen Z writers and reviewers on YouTube. They often have great insights, even if I do own T-shirts older than they are.

Chapter Fourteen: Finding Your Voice

Writing that Sings

Editors often say they're looking for that unique voice. But what does that mean? More importantly, how do you create a voice?

Voice in fiction is a combination of things. Part of it is the way the writer constructs sentences -- their verbal style. Good friends often tell me that when they read one of my books, they can hear my voice as if I'm speaking the lines. I find that true of other authors I know personally. They put together a sentence the same way whether they're writing it or saying it. It's a matter of word choice and phrasing.

But written voice also encompasses the themes that touch you as a person. For example, in Nora Roberts's romances, her stories often revolve around characters who have survived some kind of childhood abuse.

In my own fiction, dreams and nightmares are recurring elements. Characters have prophetic dreams, or dreams that reveal what they fear most. That's because I have extremely vivid dreams, so I'm acutely aware of the psychological impact a nightmare can have.

Another factor in voice is tone. Is the work light and comedic, or dark and gritty? Is the writer an optimist who sees the best in people, or a cynic who expects the worst?

The good news about all this is that I don't think your written voice is something you work at, any more than most of us "work" at our speaking voices. As you become more confident as a writer, your voice will emerge and strengthen. You will write about the things that touch you in a way that expresses your personality.

That's your voice.

Perfect Pitch Prose

That said, though, you do have to work on the writing itself. If your sentences are strings of indecipherable phrases stuck together at random, your book is simply not going to sell. No matter how complex your plot or well-developed your characters, if your writing is incoherent, your reader is not going to understand what the heck is going on.

You need to make sure your sentences are clear and concise. Don't tack on adverbs and adjectives just to show the size of your vocabulary. Readers do not care if you've memorized the entire *Oxford English Dictionary*. They just want you to entertain them. If you don't, *they won't come back.*

Sentence Length

I said earlier that I like to keep my dialogue short, with frequent interruptions from other characters. Another of my personal rules of thumb is that few sentences should be much longer than 20 words or so. Here's a scene from a very early draft of *Forever Kiss* that illustrates what I'm talking about.

Ridgemont exploded at McKinnon, swinging his sword like a scythe in a blow calculated to slice through his helm and take off the top of his head. McKinnon danced back and blocked. The shield jolted on his arm with a sound like a cannon shot, and the world pinwheeled.

The sentence lengths there are 27 words, 5 and 17. The 27-word sentence pushes the limit of length. It would read better as, "Ridgemont lunged, scything his sword right at McKinnon's head." Seven words. So I cut 20 words out of that sentence. Not only is the line shorter, it's more sharply visual.

Looking at word choice: I used "exploded" as a metaphor, but it didn't really work; people don't explode. "Swinging his sword like a scythe" became "scything" -- I wanted to keep that visual image, but the phrase was too long.

As to "slice through his helm and take off the top of his head;" if you slice through the helm, you're going to take off the top of the wearer's head, so that could go. I still didn't like "calculated," so I killed that whole phrase. The idea is to create a threat. If he's swinging the sword at McKinnon's head, the threat is there. The reader knows what will happen if the sword connects.

Look for ways to collapse your own sentences, paying particular attention to redundancy. But keep in mind the effect you're trying to create. Don't cut a sentence until it becomes weak.

I did have some good sensory detail in that paragraph. I think the sound the shield makes is good, but I wonder if it reads well. It reads as though the jolt sounds like a cannon shot, but I intended the source to be the sword: "The blade slammed into his shield with a sound like a cannon shot. The world pinwheeled as he went flying."

Putting that last phrase in its own sentence draws attention to the image and clarifies the action. What I'm trying to do is catch the feeling of being in combat. "Spun" would be shorter than "pinwheeled," but "pinwheeled" creates a particular image that "spun" doesn't. It's a longer, dizzier word, which goes with the sensation of everything spinning around you.

About the cannon shot -- though they're fighting with sword and shield, this is a contemporary story. If it had been set around the 1100s or so, I wouldn't have used the cannon metaphor, because that's too early for cannon.

Now, looking at the entire paragraph, you have:

Ridgemont lunged, scything his sword right for McKinnon's head. McKinnon danced back and blocked. The blade slammed into his shield with a sound like a cannon shot, and his arm went numb to the shoulder. The world pinwheeled as he went flying.

Notice I added a phrase, "his arm went numb to the shoulder." That's because I needed a longer sentence there; too many short sentences in a row set up a machine gun rhythm. I had his arm go numb because I wanted to show the force of the blow and work in one of the five senses.

It bothers me that I used McKinnon twice close together, but if I changed one of them to "him" or "he," it would no longer be clear whether I was talking about McKinnon or Ridgemont. Sometimes you must accept repetition to avoid confusion.

Keep in mind the implications of words, too. Alex and I didn't like the original title for the book, then called *Midnight's Master*.

I took a poll on my Yahoo loop, looking for suggestions. Somebody wrote in suggesting *Nocturnal Phantasm*. I got a couple of emails back saying, "No, that sounds like bed-wetting," and another that said, "Sounds like something teenage boys do." Privately agreeing, I thanked the lady for her suggestion.

Another reason I didn't like that suggestion was that both words are too long and too vague. In general, I like to use shorter words, because they tend to have a little more bite.

However, I also avoid words that have a lot of possible meanings. "Hit," for example, is less effective than "slam" because "hit" can mean any degree of force from a pencil hitting a table to a freight train hitting a pickup truck. "Slam," on the other hand, carries the implication of great force.

"Scything," "danced," and "jolted," are all vivid words that have a visual meaning that make you see a particular kind of movement. Look for words that do that -- and use them.

Creating A Picture With Far Fewer Than A Thousand Words

Description is key in all fiction. Good description establishes the scene in the reader's mind, providing the set the characters act upon. Without it, readers aren't sure where anyone is, and they have trouble connecting with the scene.

If you're a television and film junkie, you've probably noticed that every flick starts with a shot of the location where the story takes place. It could be the New York skyline or a log cabin in the woods. In *Star Wars*, it was that unforgettable image of an Imperial Destroyer sliding slowly by overhead, taking up the entire frame.

That's called an establishing shot, because it establishes where and when we are. It gives the viewer a framework for the story's setting.

You need to do the same thing as a writer. But like a television director, you must keep it brief. In the nineteenth century, readers would happily sit still for a two-page opening description of a sunset. Today, however, our readers are busy people raised on TikTok, and they expect you to get to the point.

As one of my readers wrote, "Yes, I need detail in descriptions. I want to be able to picture in my mind what is going on. But let's don't get carried away -- too much description can be deadly boring. Trying to fill a page with empty details snaps that concentration so it wanders. Who cares if there is change on his nightstand, or dirty socks under the bed!"

So it's a good idea to paint the scene in a few short sentences. Here's what I did in the opening prologue for *Master of the Night*.

Candlelight from the massive chandelier overhead shimmered over satin, brocade and the brilliant scarlet of British regimentals. Somebody played a violin with more vigor than skill, competing with the sound of dancing feet in the ballroom across the hall. Laughter rang out, a little too heartily from Loyalist planters, a little too smugly from the Redcoat conquerors who now occupied Charlestown.

Reece Champion sipped his wine and smiled down at the pretty Tory who was under the delusion he'd make a good husband. The square-cut décolletage of her brocade gown framed a pair of lovely breasts that would have claimed his full attention under different circumstances. As it was, though, Reece was far more interested in a conversation between two British lieutenants who stood nearby.

"By fall, Tarleton will have that Fox's tail," one of them said, his voice slurring slightly.

God, Reece loved a drunk. They made a spy's job so much easier.

My job here is to set the hook for my readers. That first paragraph is my establishing shot, telling the reader that the scene takes place during the Revolutionary War at a Loyalist ball in Charles Town, SC.

I start trying to build a sense of conflict by contrasting the too-hearty laughter of the Loyalist planters with the smug laughter of the invading Redcoats.

Next, I try to arouse the reader's curiosity. Why is Reece Champion more interested in two British officers than the pretty woman he's talking to? In the next paragraph, I reveal it's because he's a spy.

The word "spy" carries such a cargo of romance and danger, many readers will buy the book to find out what happens next.

Now, in retrospect, I did make a mistake with that book. Before that opening scene, I included a three-page prologue explaining that there's a lot more to the legend of King Arthur than anyone realizes. I shouldn't have done that, because it bogged my book down with telling instead of showing. I probably lost sales because of it.

But *Master of the Night* was my first book of the Mageverse series, and I was struggling to figure out how to clue the reader in on the complex back story. In the fourth book, *Master of Swords*, I simply showed Gawain drinking from Merlin's Grail. It was much more effective.

Again, when you have a lot of weird backstory, keep it short and deliver it in small, digestible bites. Don't choke your reader on it. Dole out details only when the reader needs to know them.

There's a simple way to determine if you've got

that kind of problem in your own work. *Read your book.*

Writing Is Rewriting

I once heard a writer I really like say she didn't do rewrites. "The way it comes out is the way I send it off."

I was incredulous. She's a good writer, but she'd be a better one if she did rewrites.

I rewrite absolutely everything. When I was a newspaper reporter, I did rewrites to clarify and sharpen 200-word crime briefs that didn't even get my byline.

No matter how good you are, your work can always be improved. Besides, you can't trust a first draft. I always find something I didn't make clear, some sentence that clunks like a rusted bell, or some bit of completely lame dialogue.

Then there are the scenes that are just too long or too short or too lacking in sensory detail. For years, I always wrote my chapters short by two pages, because I'd end up adding at least that much in the second and third drafts.

But there are some tricks to effective rewriting. When I first started out, I would try to perfect each scene before I progressed to the next. For a newbie lacking in self-confidence, this can become self-defeating fast.

If you overwork a story -- what my husband calls "polishing to the bare metal" -- you'll suck all the life out of it. In my case, I'd quickly get sick of the book, and I'd never finish it. I made that mistake for a good decade or more.

It wasn't until *The Forever Kiss* that I started forcing myself not to read the book until it was finished. I'd do my set number of pages a day, working my way through the plot. Only after I typed "The End," did I go back and reread the book.

By that point, I had forgotten what I had written in those early chapters, and I could approach it with an objective eye. I'd look for flaws, and I'd methodically fix them.

The first draft is where I establish the major plot events and conflicts. There's often very little detail in that draft, and the dialogue is flat or lacking subtext. In the second draft, I add description and massage the dialogue to create character, wit, and energy. I also like to add humor, which adds sparkle and another layer of reader interest.

Then I print out the full manuscript, because it's easier to spot problems on hard copy when you're used to reading the manuscript onscreen. I go over it with a pen, ruthlessly cutting and making notes. Working from those notes, I do the final polish.

Does anything drag? Is this description too long? Does this sentence break the momentum of the scene? If so, I don't care how clever or beautiful the bit is, out it goes.

If you want to be a professional, the work must come first. Ego doesn't even make the list of things a pro should care about.

Rewriting doesn't stop there. When my books come back from for copyedits, I often do more rewriting than the editor asks for. That's because nobody knows the effect I'm trying to achieve but me -- not even my editor. If I think a scene misses, I'm going to do my best to get it back on target.

Rewriting Traps

The problem with being a perfectionist is that you can easily become hypercritical. As my husband likes to say, "You're not just your own worst critic, you're your own sniper on the grassy knoll." Once I get to a certain point in the edits, *everything* sucks.

That's when I need another set of eyes. When I first started out, my sister read and critiqued my work. Trouble was, my sister isn't a writer. When there was a problem, she often couldn't tell me what it was.

That's when I started using other writers as critique partners. We'd critique each other's work and help one another find a book's weak spots. There are times when you get so obsessed with one approach to a story that you can't see the obvious solution to a plot problem. My CPs often tell me, "You're making this too complicated. Just do such-and-such." That's when I usually slap myself on the forehead and groan, "Why didn't I think of that?"

Because tunnel vision is an easy trap to fall into, that's why.

Agents are another line of defense. Mine was Roberta Brown, who has since retired. Since she hadn't seen the book until it was in the final draft, she could tell me if there really was a problem, or if I was just suffering from a raging case of *Everything Sucks*.

By the way, when somebody gives you feedback like this, you have to be willing to follow through. With *Master of Wolves*, I had 180 pages of the book finished when I realized there was a problem. I sent it to Roberta. She read it and said, "Your book goes off-track on page 103." My kick-ass heroine, having been bitten by a werewolf, had suddenly morphed into a whiner. I ended up gutting eighty pages and starting over. It wasn't fun, but the book was stronger for it.

May I Have Another Mistress?

I remember browsing a rather raunchy art site for

-- ahem -- research purposes, when I found a picture of a woman giving another woman a spanking. The caption was, "May I have another Mistress?"

I laughed out loud. The Phantom Comma strikes again! The artist had intended the caption to read as if the submissive was asking her mistress for another spank, but what she actually asked for was another mistress. I guess she *did* want another mistress -- that one was beating her ass!

Commas may look tiny and insignificant, but they're surprisingly powerful. A misplaced comma can completely change the meaning of a sentence in ways you don't intend. In fact, Supreme Court cases have hinged on the meaning of a comma.

So when you're addressing someone, you need a comma between the name and the rest of the sentence. "May I have another, Mistress?" Or "Mistress, may I have another?"

Commas signal the reader about what things go together in a sentence. A wonderful example is found in the title of a best-selling book on comma placement, *Eats, Shoots and Leaves* by Lynne Truss. This refers to a line the author had seen describing the habits of pandas, which eat the shoots and leaves of bamboo. But whoever had written the original line had plopped a comma after "eats," which created the impression that the panda ate, shot the waiter, and left.

If commas are your personal grammar demon, I suggest you buy a copy of *Eats, Shoots and Leaves*. Not only is it a fun read, it explains comma placement in a clear and simple way. *Sin and Syntax: How to Craft Wickedly Good Prose* by Constance Hale is another good one.

YouTube (surprise!) also has tons of tutorials that cover whatever grammatical weakness you currently have. Judging by the student work I've critiqued, I'd suggest searching on comma splices, run-on sentences, and comma placement in general.

Now, you may be thinking, "Why should I bother? That's what copy editors are for." But if you don't know proper grammar and punctuation, you're never going to get to a copy editor because your work will be rejected.

I say this *as an editor*. If I open your submission and find you don't know where to put a comma, I'm going to reject your work out of hand, even if I think your work has promise. That's because fixing your grammar would be such a massive pain in the butt, it's not worth it.

Most e-pub and freelance editors get paid a set amount per word. We don't want to waste hours and hours and *HOURS* cleaning up your mess. (Which is how long I spent on one wretched book the author hired me to edit. I'd rather clean bathroom grout with a toothbrush than fix 15,000 missing commas.) Besides, there are plenty of terrific writers who *do* know where to put a comma.

And it's not just me, either. *Every editor and agent feels the same*. We all figure if you don't know the basics of English grammar, you probably can't handle the complexities of story construction.

So if you want to become a professional writer, get thee to YouTube and learn grammar. It really isn't that damned complicated, and I'll bet you can get a handle on it if you spend a week or two watching videos.

Even if you're planning to self-publish, you still need to know spelling and grammar. When I pick up an e-book whose author doesn't know the difference between "there's" and "their's" -- which isn't even a word -- it's like listening to somebody sing off-key. I'm just not going to read that book. My life is too short to read the fictional equivalent of Roseanne Barr singing "The Star-Spangled Banner."

Admittedly, some readers don't know the rules of good grammar either, but a lot of them do. Every time those readers hit a misplaced comma or a misspelled word, it will jerk them right out of your story. They won't buy one of your books again, because you've created the impression that you're sloppy at best and poorly educated at worst.

Nor can you duck the problem by using your software's grammar or spell checker. Grammar checkers have gotten pretty good over the past 20 years, but the fact is, *computers can't read*. Checkers are easy to confuse if your sentence structure is sufficiently complex.

True, you can use a website like Grammarly or hire someone with good grammar skills to check your work. But again, you really need to know the rules if you're going to write for a living. Otherwise, every time you write an email, you'll look like an amateur.

Since my spelling is abysmal, I always run spell and grammar checks before I send a book off. It doesn't take long, and it saves me a great deal of embarrassment. Be aware though, they don't catch everything, like misused words. That's when giving your work a ruthless reread comes in handy. Double-check spellings you're not sure of -- Google is your friend.

POV

Another common problem new writers wrestle with is Point of View. That's because POV is one of those subtle, stylistic effects most readers aren't consciously aware of. New writers don't realize it's a problem because they've never really noticed it in the work of others.

Any scene in a book should be seen through the eyes of a character in the story. Yeah, you can have an omniscient point of view -- meaning the reader becomes a godlike observer. But that will kill the emotional involvement you feel when you're in the point of view of someone with skin in the game.

Handling POV is easier in first person narratives. That kind of POV is obvious -- it's the "I" who's telling you the story. "I did this," or "I did that."

But until recently, few romances used first person, since it deprives you of the POV of one of the protagonists. If you're in the POV of the heroine, you have no way of knowing how the hero really feels about her. That can work -- it's a great way to add tension. But if you want to share the hero's experience of falling in love, you won't get it from the heroine's POV.

As a result, it's become popular to alternate -- one scene from the hero's, the next from the heroine's, while labeling each scene break with the character's name. I've used that format myself, and it makes a great change of pace.

Things get a little more complicated when you're in third person, the traditional POV of romance.

Maybe the viewpoint character is the heroine, or the convenience store clerk who watches your hero walk in to pay for his gas. But whoever it is, you should stick to that one point of view until the scene is over. Switching POV in mid-scene is called "head-hopping," and it's considered a deadly technical sin because it tends to give readers psychic whiplash.

First, they're in the hero's point of view, then a

paragraph later, the author has switched to the heroine's, or maybe his dog's. Readers have to figure out whose head they're in, which can be seriously confusing.

Anytime you confuse the reader, she's going to have to stop, reread and figure out what's going on. That's bad, because if she stops, she might remember she's got to go do the laundry. Maybe she'll even forget to pick your book up again after she's done. That in turn may mean you won't make her autobuy list, so no future sales for you.

Don't head-hop. Decide on a viewpoint character and stick to that character for the entire scene.

But how do you decide on the best viewpoint character for a given scene? It should be whoever is affected most by what happens. If your hero is getting the crap beaten out of him, you want to see the scene through his eyes. On the other hand, if watching the hero get his clock cleaned makes the heroine realize she loves him, you may want to be in her point of view instead.

Do remember, however, that you can show only what that character would logically know. You can't have a paragraph like, "What Danielle didn't realize is there was a bomb under her seat." That's called "authorial intrusion," and it's bad.

What you might want to do instead is show the bomber watching Danielle walk through the train and sit down. Maybe he gets an erection, just thinking about the bomb under her seat. Then he gets up and strolls off the train as if he's in no hurry at all.

That's a heck of a lot more chilling than, "What Danielle didn't realize is there was a bomb under her seat."

Another other common mistake is showing

something the POV character can't see. For example, when you're in your hero's point of view, avoid lines like "His eyes darkened in reaction." He can't see his own eyes, so he has no way of knowing his eyes darken. Describe only what the character can see and feel. "My hands curled into fists" is fine because the character can feel her hands fisting. Or he can realize he's blushing because his cheeks are getting hot.

Now, when it comes to the one-POV-per-scene rule, there are some exceptions. In fight scenes and love scenes, I often want to know what both characters are experiencing.

When you need to switch POVs, find a stopping point in the scene, skip a space, and pick up with the new point of view. Use the viewpoint character's name in the first line, along with a sensation he's feeling:

Pain throbbed in Kel's skull with a beat he could feel in his teeth. Slowly, he opened his eyes to a blurry vision of darkening sky overhead. He blinked and managed to focus.

This paragraph establishes whose viewpoint we're in. There's no guesswork involved, so the reader doesn't have to stop and figure anything out.

However, you should not do point of view shifts like this very often -- no more than once every three or four pages. More frequently would be too jarring.

It's a good idea to read back over your book after you've given it a chance to "cool." A week or so away from it should be long enough to give you a little more objectivity. If you hit a patch that throws you while you're reading, you need to take it apart and fix whatever's wrong.

Chapter Fifteen: Writing Short and Going Long

Novellas, Short Stories, and Series Novels

I started my career in short fiction, first in comic books, then writing erotic romance novellas for Red Sage's *Secrets* anthology series. This really worked to my advantage. To succeed in fiction, you need to learn how to craft strong characters with powerful conflicts that play out through the story's beginning, middle, and end. Then you need to know how to polish the story with crisp, clear writing. That's a lot easier to do in a 25,000-word novella than a 100,000-word novel -- especially for someone like me who had trouble finishing a book.

If you're a newbie, I advise you to start with short stories, then tackle a novella before you attempt that novel. (Especially since your first story is likely to suck. It's less heartbreaking to have to toss a novella than a novel.) What's more, there are plenty of e-publishing markets for erotic romance shorts that will help you get your foot in the door of publication.

Even more importantly, you can start building an audience. One reason Berkley editor Cindy Hwang approached me about writing for her was that I had already built a name for myself at Red Sage. I'd written seven novellas, a novel, and a whole bunch of comic books, and I knew how to construct a story. I also had a fan following. So she wasn't buying a pig in a poke.

Short Plots

In general, the shorter the fiction, the more tightly you need to plot it before you start writing. When I was working in comics, I knew I had only 22 pages per book. Not 23, not 20, *exactly* 22. I had to know what took place on every single page of the script before I sat down to write. And I made sure I did.

But writing short fiction is more than a matter of tight plotting. You must scale down everything from the cast to the conflicts. My novellas have a hero, a heroine, a villain, and a couple of walk-ons to help set up the conflict. Even then, the novella bounds along at a good clip. Getting all those people and three sex scenes into such a short length is not easy.

And, of course, engineering an HEA within 25,000 words is a bear. It's helpful if your hero and heroine have a past romantic history. If you're writing a short story, giving them a past is a necessity, because there's just no time for a couple of strangers to fall in love. You just can't pull it off, no matter how good you are.

Now, I've gotten strangers to love in a novella, but I also cheat. Because I write paranormals, I can have the hero and heroine form a psychic bond that makes falling in love a little more believable. (Assuming you're willing to believe in the idea of a psychic bond, anyway.)

As far as the external conflict goes, that can be another serious challenge in a novella. I usually do have one, because I like to write that kind of story. I rarely write novellas that are nothing but romantic conflict. Three of them are "Candidate for the Kiss," and "Kissing the Hunter" in *Forever Kisses Vol. 2* and "Bound by the Dream" in *Captive Dreams*. I like "Bound by the Dream" and "Kissing the Hunter" because the conflicts between the two couples are so intense. Unfortunately, I'm not sure "Candidate" works quite as well.

That said, there's a trick to external conflict in a novella, because you can't let it overwhelm the romance. And it will, given half the chance.

First, the conflict needs to be something simple: catch the bad guy, retrieve the stolen whatsit. Notice that ending world hunger is not on the list. Any complex problem is going to be too much for the length.

Second, you need to keep the bad guy out of the picture for most of the novella. Maybe the antagonist shows up in Chapter One, and again for the climactic fight at the end, but other than that, keep them offstage. You need to devote those middle chapters to getting your characters to love.

Which brings me to sex. Another major challenge of an erotic romance is getting two strangers in the sack within hours of meeting each other.

As I mentioned earlier, you have to motivate it. In "Moon Dance," my novella in *Over the Moon*, my werewolf heroine needs to get pregnant, so she seeks out my werewolf cop hero for both baby-making and protection from the bad guy.

I needed to give her a good reason for this, or she would have looked calculating. So the novella's first scene was her fighting off her abusive would-be fiancé. I then establish that only by getting pregnant can she avoid being forced to marry the creep werewolf. There's a lot going on in "Moon Dance," but I think I managed to wrap everything up in a neat little ball by the end.

What you *don't* want to do is establish an external conflict and then abandon it in favor of having sex. I've seen this done in a novella or two, and it's never good. You don't want the reader asking, "But what about the one-legged killer clown in Chapter One?"

If you just want your characters to have lots of

sex, come up with a conflict built solely around the bedroom and drop the external conflict. It will leave the reader much less frustrated in the end.

When it comes to very short erotic romance -- 12,000 words or less -- you *have* to build your conflict solely around sex, because that's all there's room for. That means the hero and heroine *must* have a romantic history. Basically, they should already be in love when the story begins, but something has torpedoed the relationship. Your job is to resolve whatever is keeping them apart.

I once did an unpublished story I liked a great deal with this kind of conflict. The heroine is a genetically engineered mercenary warrior who is captured by an enemy commander. To her surprise, he turns out to be the same man who had once been her human lover.

When she'd been just a stupid eighteen-year-old, she'd dumped him because he was too human. She's been kicking herself ever since.

In the meantime, however, he's become a vampire, and he's still really pissed off about being dumped. Lots of sex ensues, and they finally clear the air and get the HEA they've both been wanting for fifteen years.

Dirt-simple plot, perfect for the length.

Going Really, Really Long

At the other end of the length spectrum is the romantic series romance.

In most genres, a series follows the same character through various adventures. Sherlock Holmes is probably the most famous series hero. This is much harder to pull off in romance, because romances are about one couple finding each other and falling in love. If you've got an HEA at the end of the first book, there's nothing to drive the rest of the series, unless you break the couple up in the next book. But you can't keep doing that either; the reader gets tired of it pretty fast.

Then there's the way Nora Roberts handled the *In Death* series. Technically, these books are futuristic police procedural mysteries, though they're often shelved as romance. Romance is an integral part of the plot, though, since much of the heat comes from the marriage of Eve Dallas and her rich, handsome husband Roarke. The two butt heads as they work to solve murders together. The dynamic is interesting, because in a turnabout on the usual pattern, Eve is the cop.

Once the couple's relationship was solid, Roberts started introducing B romances between secondary characters, like Eve's partner Peabody and her e-detective lover, McNab.

In Death, however, is the only romance series I can think of that currently follows this pattern. Authors more typically design a romance series around the romantic adventures of a group of sisters, brothers, or friends, marrying each of the characters off in successive books. Readers love this form, because they get a chance to meet the heroes and heroines ahead of time and anticipate the books to come.

Whenever you can capture readers like this, you have guaranteed sales. A new reader picks up one of the books, likes it, and goes looking for the earlier books. I've seen this at work myself. Whenever a new book in the Berkley Mageverse series came out, the others would start appearing on Amazon's Top 100 Romances List, even though those books had fallen off the list months before.

Villains are another problem for a series romance writer. In my case, I used an old comic book trick, the story arc. This is a conflict that extends over several books, is resolved, and is then replaced by another conflict. Again, this form is good for sales, because readers want to get the previous books to see how the whole thing started.

However, be careful you don't end up with an anticlimax. If your couple is pursuing a villain throughout the book and doesn't catch him, you run the risk of disappointing your readers.

I ducked that issue in the Mageverse series by giving each book its own henchman villain who worked for the overall Big Bad.

My problem is avoiding the Superman syndrome. That's where you make a hero so powerful, ordinary humans pose absolutely no threat to him. You must give the protagonist his Kryptonite -- a weakness his human Lex Luthor can use to level the playing field.

In the first arc, I took care of that by giving my villains magical powers, but I killed those villains off. So I had to create a whole new kind of bad guy: a werewolf called Warlock, who also had magical abilities and some truly nasty flunkies.

There's yet another problem with writing a long-running series: writer fatigue. This happened even to Arthur Conan Doyle, creator of Sherlock Holmes, who killed off his immortal detective in one book because he'd gotten sick of him. Readers were so enraged, Doyle ended up bringing Sherlock back.

At some point, even the best writer simply runs out of ideas.

One way to avoid writer fatigue is to start a new series and alternate it and the old one. That lets you remain fresh and maintain your interest in the concept. And if you can stay interested, your readership will be too.

Chapter Sixteen: Finding Your Book a Home

Word Count And Other Vital Details

Word count -- a publisher's required length of a given work -- is a far more important subject than most newbies realize. Every publisher from the legacy Big Five in New York to small e-publishers like Changeling have hard and fast word counts dictated by their bottom line.

When I was publishing with Berkley, the required word count was 100,000 words, which is the standard length of a paperback novel. That length meant the resulting paperback would have a standard number of pages so the company knew what the cost would be to print and ship it to bookstores.

E-publishers don't print or ship anything, but they still have production costs. They need to pay for editing and formatting the book, which is based on word count. If a book is too expensive because of its length and readers don't buy it, the publisher loses money.

When you decide to look for a publisher, your first act must be to check their submission page. Do they publish the kind of book you've written?

For example, Changeling Press publishes erotic romance for a largely adult female audience, including Heterosexual and LGBTQA+, Multiple Partner, and Sex and Gender Shifting themes. That means you do not want to submit your YA or Christian inspirational novel, because we don't publish those, and you'd be wasting everyone's time. I don't care if it's the next Harry Potter; we can't do a damn thing with it.

By the same token, you don't want to send your BDSM Romance to a Christian Inspirational publisher, because that's not what they do. So it's to your benefit to go to the submission page of the publisher and check what they're looking for (Submissions Guidelines can generally be found under **HELP**, **About Us**, or **Submissions Guidelines**). Changeling Submission Guidelines

Sometimes even after you have a contract with a publisher, their needs change. I did very well with Berkley -- even making *The New York Times, USA Today*, and *Publisher's Weekly* bestseller lists -- until the Great Recession took out half the brick-and-mortar bookstores in the country. The publishing industry decided paranormal romance was no longer hot, and the majority of the paranormal authors I knew lost their contracts. Berkley asked me to write contemporary romances, but that wasn't something I was interested in. Changeling became my primary publisher.

Make sure you pick a publisher who publishes the kind of book you've written.

By the way, finish the book *before* you send in a proposal so it will be ready to go if they ask for it.

Cover Letters, Queries, And Proposals

Even before you've finished your book, figure out which publishers or agents you're targeting by checking the submission guidelines on their website. Follow them on social media like *YouTube, Facebook, X,* and *TikTok,* and subscribe to their newsletter.

Search for editors or agents who are acquiring. You want young ones who haven't yet established a stable of authors. Follow their socials, but don't harass them about your book. Just read what they have to say, paying particular attention to what they're interested in and looking for. They'll probably mention the books they've edited or represented. Read those, searching for books similar to the one you've written.

By the time the book is finished, you should have a good idea which agent or editor might be interested in it.

Send them an email query with a brief description of your book. Some agents or publishers will want you to send them a proposal consisting of the first fifty pages and a synopsis, which summarizes the book's plot. (You'll find the synopsis of *Master of the Moon* in the appendix of this book.)

Your cover letter might say something like this:

"You'll find enclosed the first fifty pages of my completed 100,000-word time travel romance, *Jane's Warlord*. Newspaper reporter Jane Colby is investigating a series of brutal murders when Baran Arvid shows up at her house claiming to be a warrior from the future sent to protect her. She thinks he's nuts until his talking cyborg wolf foils her escape attempt.

"Jane and Baran form a passionate alliance as they hunt a time traveling serial killer. Their growing love only complicates the fight. Both know Baran will have to return to the future -- assuming they survive their battle with the killer once known as Jack the Ripper."

Then toss in a couple of lines about yourself and your qualifications. For example, I might have included the fact that I based *Jane* on my own experiences as a newspaper reporter who covered murders in a small town. You don't need to go into a description of your family or your dog or the fact you've wanted to be published since you were nine. The editor doesn't care.

If you've won any writing awards or contests, mention those. If you're a member of a writer's organization like *Passionate Ink*, mention that. If you've been published in a magazine, e-book, or small press, that deserves mention too. But keep it under a page.

Next, include your synopsis. (There's one in the appendix if you'd like to see how it's done.) The synopsis length will vary according to publisher, so check the publisher or agent's guidelines. Make sure to include how you resolve all your conflicts, external and internal.

Finally, include the first 50 pages of your book, roughly the first two or three chapters. Hopefully, the editor will write back asking for the whole thing.

Then email it and go work on something else so you won't go crazy while you wait. And you will wait, likely for months, so don't get impatient.

In the meantime, write another book.

Section Six -- Practicalities
Contracts, Editors, Agents, and Marketing

Chapter Seventeen: Stupid Writer Tricks
Or, How I Spent Twenty Years Shooting Myself in the Foot

I once heard myself referred to as an overnight success. After all, I published my first novel with Berkley Publishing in June, 2004. Three months later, one of my novellas hit the *New York Times* list as part of an anthology called *Hot Blooded*. (Christine Feehan, Maggie Shayne and Emma Holly were the other authors, so it's no surprise that book was a hit.) A month later, *Master of the Night,* my third book, made the *USA Today* list. In May, 2005, my fourth book occupied spots on the *USA Today* list for three weeks. That same month, I won the Critics Choice for Best Erotic Romance from Romantic Times Bookclub Magazine. A month later, Christine Feehan, Maggie Shayne, Emma Holly and I received the Borders Bestselling Anthology Award for *Hot Blooded*.

In August, 2005, Berkley published *Mercenaries*, a trade paperback anthology of three of my futuristic novellas. It went on to spend three weeks as number 1 on the Barnes and Noble trade paperback romance list. In April, 2006, *Master of Wolves* hit the *Publisher's Weekly*, *USA Today* and *New York Times* Extended bestseller lists. In October, 2006, *Master of Swords* made the lists too.

I've got to admit, that certainly sounds like overnight success, but the reality is far different. It took me twenty years to do all that because I kept shooting myself in the foot in an impressive variety of ways. You name an idiot mistake they tell you not to make, and I made it.

I will now explain them all to you in hopes you

can avoid doing the same boneheaded things.

Finish The Book

You can't sell a book you don't finish. For years, I was enormously intimidated by the thought of writing 400 pages. Being a perfectionist, I'd write a chapter, and then I'd start rewriting it. I'd polish and polish, and soon I'd get sick of the book, convince myself it sucked, and go start another book. I only broke this cycle when I learned not to polish until I got the book finished. (I only go back and rewrite if I've gone completely off-track, which does sometime happen.) In fact, I try not to read the book until I get it finished.

Creative writing and editing are done by completely different parts of the brain. If you turn on your internal editor too soon, it will nitpick your book to death. Don't do that. Instead:

A. Plot the book out ahead of time, or at least get some idea where you're going.

B. Write something every single day. If you write five pages a day, you'll have the first draft in less than three months.

C. Then and only then, do you start editing. Go through the book looking for stuff that doesn't work, and fix those things. If you haven't tried to read the book during the writing process, it will have cooled enough that you can judge it objectively.

Be ruthless. Cut anything that doesn't contribute to advancing the plot, characterization, or conflict. If it doesn't do anything except sound pretty, kill it. Then, if you're not on deadline, let the book sit a month while you think about the next book. (If you are on deadline, you probably can't wait that long.)

Finally, give the book a third rewrite, cleaning up typos and grammatical errors and anything you haven't fixed the first time around. After that, send it off.

A Good Critique Partner Is Worth Her Weight In Gold

If you can find a good critique partner who understands your genre and whose judgment you trust, work with her through the writing process. I've already talked about how my CPs point out problems in my work and helped me brainstorm solutions. Often the answer is staring me right in the face, but I'm too blocked to see it.

Grow a Pair

Rejection letters are not fun. There's nothing as painful as going through the whole writing process and sending a book to a publisher only to receive a rejection letter six months later.

Do it anyway.

I wrote and finished my first book in 1990. I waited more than a year while it sat on somebody's desk at Harlequin before it was finally rejected. Brenda Chin wrote me a rejection letter saying something to the effect of, "My test reader really liked this book, but I think it's terrible." She went on to say it was clichéd and unbelievable.

I really need to send Ms. Chin a thank you note,

because she was right. It sucked. I'm glad Harlequin didn't publish it, because I would hate to have that piece of crap out in the world. It's currently hiding in my sock drawer.

In hindsight, what I should have done was sit down and immediately write another book, taking Ms. Chin's criticism to heart. Then I should have sent it to her. The fact that she took the time to write a personal note meant she did see something promising in that God-awful book. Otherwise, she'd have sent a form rejection letter.

Instead, I piddled around for the next several years, never finishing anything until I finally turned forty and decided to quit screwing around. Within a few months of getting that first book finished, I had a contract. If I'd gotten off my duff sooner, I suspect I would have been published years earlier than I was.

So write the book and submit it. If it's rejected, submit it to somebody else. In the meantime, write something new. Keep writing. Remember: writing is a learning process, and you learn by screwing up. Odds are, your first book is going to be so bad as to be unpublishable, but your next will be better, and the one after that, better still. After a while, you'll be damned good.

E-Pubs Are Your Friends

That's one reason I like e-pubs and small presses as the best places to get started. New York publishing is the equivalent of the Major Leagues in baseball. E-pubs and small presses are the minor leagues. They give you the opportunity to work with editors and hone the skills you need to succeed on a national print level.

New York editors generally expect you to know

what you're doing by the time you get to them, and they're not going to take the time to work with an amateur. They'll just reject you. E-pubs and small presses will take that time, helping you get ready for the big leagues.

However, please note that I am not implying that people who are only e-pubbed can't make it in New York. I know many excellent e-published or self-published authors who are more than up to Major League standards. The big houses simply haven't realized it yet.

Start Short

It's easier to learn how to structure a narrative if you start with a 25,000-word novella instead of a 100,000-word novel. A novel is a very complicated structure, and there are a lot of things you must get just right.

Writing fiction is like juggling. It's much easier to start with just two balls instead of ten.

Research the Market

When you decide to go for publication, look at what your target publisher is doing. Read a bunch of that publisher's books. See if you're interested in doing what they publish. Don't send something to a publisher that's completely unsuitable, like submitting an erotic romance to a Christian inspirational publisher. That's just asking to get your book handed back to you, smoking at the end of a skewer.

Write What You're Best At

One thing I did right was look at what I wrote and figure out what I did well. When I re-read my first attempts at romance, I could see my work was extremely labored. The only thing that sparkled was the sex scenes.

So when I learned Red Sage was acquiring sexy novellas in 1995, I instantly knew this was a publisher I could write for. I wrote a novella called "Roarke's Prisoner," and publisher Alexandria Kendall bought it within a month of my sending it in. I went on to write seven novellas and a novel for Red Sage.

What's more, Cindy Hwang at Berkley read one of my *Secrets* novellas for pleasure and emailed me, asking if I'd like to submit something to her. Why? The market was finally publishing what I loved to write.

Despite Everything I Just Told You -- Send In Three Chapters And An Outline

This bit of advice comes from Jayne Ann Krentz, by the way. She says query letters are a waste of time, because nobody can judge your writing from a query. Instead, send in the first three chapters and an outline.

Krentz maintains it's human nature to read that first page of the story. If you can get them on the first page, they'll want to see the rest.

Agents Are A Lot Easier To Acquire Once You've Got A Publisher's Interest

After Cindy Hwang said she wanted to buy my book, I got online and asked if anyone knew any agents. Emma Holly, another *Secrets* alumna, suggested her agent, Roberta Brown. I contacted Roberta, and within a month I had both a publisher and an agent. I needed Roberta, because as I am about to explain, I am a wuss. Roberta got me much more money than I would have ever had the guts to ask for.

Never, Ever, *Ever* Work Without A Contract

If somebody offers to publish your stuff but refuses to give you a contract, run far, far away.

In 1986, I sent one of my short stories to a comic book convention with my sister, who gave it to a black-and-white comic book publisher. (Meaning, the book was printed in black and white, as opposed to the standard four-color books like *Batman*.) He read it, liked it, and offered to publish a comic book mini-series based on it. He did not, however, offer a contract.

The verbal agreement was that the publisher, the artist, and I would jointly own the copyright and split any profits. I, being twenty-five and dumb as a box of rocks, agreed.

I spent the next several months working with a fantastic editor, who taught me the nuts and bolts of writing fiction while I wrote three comic book scripts. I then went on to write nine more scripts over the next year for three more mini-series. We published the first series in 1987, and it went number 3 on the black-and-white list for the nation, so we published a hardcover version in 1988.

I got one check for $3,000 and never received another dime.

Immediately afterward, the black-and-white market collapsed, and the publisher shelved the nine books I'd spent more than a year writing. I didn't make one penny off any of those books. Not a kill fee, nothing. (Of course, the publisher lost money too, since he'd already paid the artists, letterers, and inkers.)

A couple of years went by, and I decided to publish my books with someone else, but my first publisher refused to allow it. Most contracts include clauses that allow a work to revert to the author's control if the publisher does nothing with it. That would have been a very nice thing to have. But again, no contract, so I was screwed.

In 1993 the publisher decided to try selling the series to the movies. *Then* he produced a contract, which I stupidly signed. The film rights never sold.

When I hit it big with Berkley ten years later and got the idea to publish a science fiction version of the book, he told me I'd have to pay him and the artist a licensing fee to use my own characters. Which killed that idea.

However, I don't really regret working with him, because he did give me that wonderful editor who taught me how to write. Still, I should never have agreed to work without a contract.

Never Ever Agree To Work For A Share Of Net Profits -- There Won't Be Any

Several years later, I made a similar rotten deal with an e-pub that wanted to publish one of my books in Print on Demand form. Now, POD is very expensive, so I agreed to get a percentage of whatever profits there were from the book.

Then my monthly royalty statements started coming in. I would make $120 or so off 100 copies of the e-book version of the title, but I'd make only $24 off all 110 copies of the POD. That's even worse when you consider they were selling the e-book for $6 and the POD for $15. I was actually losing money by selling the POD version.

The fact is, when you agree to work for net profit, they can claim anything and everything as a cost of publication. I'm not saying that's what this publisher did, but it was a bad deal, and I should never have signed it. *Only work for a percentage of gross -- the actual cover cost of the book.*

By the way, if they have a clause in the contract you don't like, and then verbally promise not to exercise the clause, don't believe them. They'll eventually exercise the clause anyway. This has happened to me.

There's a saying in Hollywood: a verbal agreement is not worth the paper it's written on. You're just asking to get screwed.

And you will be.

Never Sign A Contract With An Excessive Expiration Date

At one point, an e-publisher was trying to get me to sign a contract for the life of the copyright. The life of the copyright, by the way, is 75 years after you're dead. By then, I had learned a thing or two, and I didn't sign the contract. Then they wanted me to sign one with an expiration of seven years, and again I refused.

If a big New York publisher offers you such a deal, that's one thing -- as long as the rights revert if they let the book go out of print. But do not sign that kind of contract with an e-pub.

If you sign a contract with an expiration date that's too long, you can't sell it to another publisher, should one make the offer. In my case, Berkley bought all my e-books for one of my publishers, and I was able to make thousands more on them than I ever would have seen otherwise.

Before You Sign

If possible, get a lawyer, agent or other knowledgeable person to look at your contract before you sign it. Sometimes contracts that look perfectly straight-forward can contain hidden traps. When we were negotiating the sale of one of my e-books to Berkley, there was a clause in the e-pub's contract that could have blocked Berkley from translating the book. We had to get a release from the e-pub, which involved groveling on my part. Given my history with that particular e-pub, groveling was not something I enjoyed.

Luckily, even if you don't have an agent or lawyer, you can find other professional authors online who may be willing to help you. Ask one of them.

Be Conservative In The Deadlines You Agree To

Don't commit yourself to deadlines that are too close together. You may be able to write 400 pages in 40 days, but I guarantee that there will be days when you'll get stuck. It's much better to give yourself a lot more time than you think you'll need than to have to ask for an extension. I'm bad about over-committing myself, and it always gets me in trouble.

Don't Quit Your Day Job

It's common wisdom among writers that you should wait until you've got a couple of years of royalties coming in before you quit your day job.

I knew that rule. I quit anyway, because my boss was driving me nuts. I then spent the next year being forced to borrow money from my father to get by. The royalties finally started coming in a year later. Had I waited, my life would have been much less stressful.

Be aware that though many e-pubbed authors have made very good money over time, there's a trick to it: you have to have a huge back list. That's a minimum of ten books, which will take time to write. You've got to be able to support yourself in the meantime. Again, don't quit your day job.

When the money does start coming in, pay your taxes on a quarterly basis. Once you go to work for a major publisher and start making real money, pay your estimated taxes every quarter, just as the IRS requires. (That's because writers are considered independent contractors, so publishers don't take taxes out of your check the way a regular employer does. What's more, you also have to pay the employer's portion of Social Security as well as the employee half.)

I realize this can be painful -- particularly if you're worried about going broke -- but if you wait until April 15, you could find yourself with a huge tax bill. That's happened to me, and it's not fun. Then you've got penalties and interest to deal with. Again, not fun.

Talk to a tax professional for advice on what to do, and start putting money aside. You'll be glad you did.

Chapter Eighteen: Pseudonyms

For many erotic romance authors, a pseudonym -- pen name -- is a necessity for a variety of reasons. First, there's concern about the reaction of friends or family members who may disapprove of a woman writing anything so blatantly sexy. You may even be justifiably worried about losing your day job.

That was true in my case. When I first started writing erotic romance for Red Sage, I was working for a religious broadcaster. I knew I'd be fired if my employer discovered what I was doing.

Another issue is my real last name, Woodcock, which is perhaps a little too apt for an erotic romance author. I once mentioned this to my Yahoo list, and one of my readers just hooted in disbelief. "Oh, I know that's not your real name!" Uh, yeah. It is.

In 2006, I did an interview with a snarky little reporter who called me "Woodpenis" in his story. I'll spare you my reaction to that witticism.

A more serious concern is the issue of stalkers. It's not unusual for erotic romance authors to find male convicts among their readership. It's therefore a good idea to use a pen name to make it a little more difficult for some nutball to find you.

You may even want to get a post office box in another town and have your mail forwarded to you. When you start running contests and promotions, you'll eventually have to send out prizes to strangers. You may not want your home address on that envelope. A P.O. box will give you peace of mind.

Choosing the Right Pen Name

When choosing a pseudonym, don't pick one that sounds like a stripper's stage name. For some reason, e-pub authors are prone to do this. I, for example, briefly used Anastasia Day, which sounds like someone who would wear pasties to work.

Imagine saying, "I want to talk to you about having more respect for erotic romance writers. My name? Oh, I'm Stormy Dawn."

You want a name that says you're a professional, and you expect to be treated like one. Mary Jo Putney tells authors to use their real first name with a made-up last. I can tell you from personal experience, this is a really good idea.

In my case, my sister's first name is Angela. As I said, she was my first reader when I started out, so I named my pseudonym after her. (The last name came from my favorite High School English teacher, Beverly Knight.)

Now, when I first started writing for Red Sage, I wasn't concerned about confusing people, because it was the 1990s and I didn't come in contact with fans.

Then I got a Yahoo group. At first, I used my real name when signing emails, but new members didn't realize I was Angela Knight. So I started signing everything with my pen name.

After getting my Berkley contract, I was invited to the Berkley cocktail party at that year's RWA conference. I spent the entire party saying, "Hello, my name is Julie Woodcock, and I write as Angela Knight." That's a confusing mouthful, so I finally simplified it to Angela Knight. Now that's all I use when dealing with fans, other writers, and almost everyone in publishing.

Trouble is, I have to remember to respond when somebody says, "Hey, Angela!" I want to look around for my sister.

So use your first name as part of your

pseudonym.

Oh, by the way -- *do not* let your publisher slip in a contract clause saying they own your pen name. If you do, you won't be able to take your pseudonym with you when you move to another publisher. That means you'll have to build your readership all over again, and you don't want to do that. Harlequin was once notorious for that.

Remember that the lawyer who wrote your contract was working for the publisher, not you. Read that thing carefully before you sign it.

Chapter Nineteen: Writer Etiquette
Dealing with Editors, Agents, Reviewers and Readers

Writing is an artistic activity, but being a writer is a profession. Painters may be able to afford artistic temperament and flights of bitchiness, because all they need to produce their work is a canvas and paints. Hopefully, someone will pay good money for that one-off painting.

You, however, need a publisher, because books are not one-off propositions.

A publisher is neither the manager of the Taco Bell where you worked when you were seventeen, nor your personal fairy godmother making all your dreams come true. He or she is an investor and business partner who mass produces your work and distributes it to customers.

And it's not a cheap investment, either. Back in the early 2000s, it cost a New York publisher between $75,000 and $80,000 to publish the average mass market romance. That's aside from the advance. That cost includes editing and designing the book, printing, binding, marketing, and distributing it to stores. (I tried to Google the current price but got buried in paid ads for scammers looking to target authors who want to self-publish.)

If you're an editor, your job is to find a book that will earn back that cost, plus a profit. If the book doesn't manage to "earn out" -- making not only its production costs, but the cost of the author's advance -- it's a black mark against both the writer and the editor who bought the book. Enough black marks, and you won't be an editor anymore.

And the writer won't be offered another contract.

There are other ways an editor can get into trouble. If an author doesn't deliver her book on time, the editor can find herself with an ugly hole in her production schedule and nothing to fill it with. If she can't find a replacement, the publisher's sales take a hit. That's not going to make the boss happy.

If the book comes in needing massive rewrites because it's poorly written, the production schedule may be placed in jeopardy again. If the writer turns diva on her long-suffering editor, refusing to do needed rewrites because they don't suit her "artistic vision," there's yet another nasty problem.

In short, what a smart editor is looking for is not only a damn good book, but a professional writer who hits her deadlines. She wants somebody willing to take the time and trouble to edit her own work ahead of time so it will need minimal copy edits. If there's a problem with a book, she wants a writer who listens to her and fixes that problem instead of refusing on the grounds of "artistic vision."

She wants someone willing to write not just one good book, but dozens and dozens, each one making a fatter profit than the next. That's the kind of author that can make an editor's career.

By the way, don't bother submitting to a senior editor at a house. She's already got a stable of best-selling authors. Choose a junior editor, because she's more likely to be hungry and searching for a hot talent that could make her career. Check publishers' websites for lists of editors.

You must then convince that editor you're the writer she's looking for. That means turning in a query letter or proposal free of errors, grammatical and otherwise.

Don't try to be too clever with your cover letter either. When I told my agent I was writing this book, she laughed and said, "Don't start your cover letter by saying, 'If you've never had an orgasm, you don't want this book.' She'd gotten a query with just that snarky opening the week before.

If you wouldn't say it at a job interview, don't say it in a cover letter.

As a new author, you'd be advised to have your book already completed and ready to send the minute you get the word the editor wants it. What's more, that book needs to be absorbing and well-written, as well as highly marketable.

And no, none of that is easy. But the rewards are more than worth it.

Presenting Yourself

One good way to meet editors and get invited to submit your work is to attend writers' conferences, especially those which list editors as speakers. Sign up for "pitch" interviews. If the editor likes your description of your work, she'll invite you to submit.

First, sign up for the conference early and obtain a pitch appointment as soon as you can, because slots fill up fast.

Next, work up a little 25-word blurb to describe your book, something similar to what you'd read on the back of a paperback. Unlike a paperback, however, you want to reveal how you resolve the conflict. Don't tell the editor, "If you want to find out how it ends, you have to buy the book." Uh, no, actually, she doesn't. Saying such a thing would instantly result in your being struck off her list of potential authors, because you've just revealed yourself as an amateur.

By the same token, if you encounter an editor in

the ladies' room, do not slide your manuscript printout under the stall door. Again, this does not create the professional image you want. It just says, "Hey, I'm rude!"

If you encounter an editor roaming around, you can certainly be friendly and talk to her just as you would any other human being. Friends of mine have done this -- and have been invited to submit their work, much to their delight.

One interesting pitch approach is to create a brief Powerpoint presentation about your book. It should take no more than five or ten minutes, hitting the highlights of the characters, the plot, and its resolution. Make sure to mention the characters' internal and external conflicts too.

Diane Whiteside successfully pitched her book to Brava editor Kate Duffy using that approach. She didn't take the laptop to the pitch with her -- she said that would have been as bad as taking the manuscript. But she did use it to work out her timing and delivery.

Dress for Success

Remember, this is a professional business interview, and you need to dress accordingly. Leave the leather pants and bustier at home. Costumes may make great theater for your fans, but they don't inspire confidence in an editor. Wear conservative business clothing and understated makeup and jewelry.

I know you're an erotic romance author, but that only means you need to be even more painstaking in creating a professional impression. You may write steamy romance, but you're not a bimbo, and you expect to be treated with respect.

Most importantly, if you're invited to submit your manuscript, turn it in. Pitches can be frustrating to editors, because a surprising number of would-be authors never actually follow up with a submission. That's why you really need to have the book finished before you pitch it. When you get home, email it.

You may have to wait six months or so to hear anything back. Be patient. If six months go by and you haven't heard, it's acceptable to write a polite query whether or not the book is still being considered.

If you get a rejection letter, look at the kind of rejection it is. If it's a form letter, that means the editor wasn't impressed. A rejection that mentions what you did wrong is usually a sign that she saw potential, even if she felt the work wasn't quite there. If she makes direct suggestions about how to fix the book, rewrite accordingly and submit it to her again. If she indicates she'd like to see another project instead, send her another project.

After Acceptance

If and when you finally get The Call from an editor saying she wants your book, take a deep breath and resist the impulse to scream, "YES!" Tell her you're interested, but you need to think about it a little. Then head to one of the online writing groups on Facebook or TikTok and ask if anyone knows about this publisher or if they can suggest an agent. Again, this is where networking is crucial.

You want a good agent with a good reputation, not one of the fly-by-night kind who charge fees for reading manuscripts. Stay far, far away from anybody like that. You want an agent who makes her money by selling books to editors, not by preying on hapless newbies.

Traditionally, publishers send checks to agents, who then send the checks to you. That means a bad agent can steal you blind, and believe me, it's happened to some very big names.

By the way, you can request split accounting, where you get your check and the agent gets hers for her fifteen percent. This saves everybody the hassle.

Once you get some recommendations, call the agents and explain you have a publisher's interest. Ask if the agent will represent you. That's what I did, and I haven't regretted it. From the start, my agent got me significantly more money than I would have gotten on my own.

The other advantage to having an agent is that you can let her be the heavy in negotiations. That way, you and your editor can maintain a nice, professional relationship without the strain of money conversations.

Which brings me to advances.

Don't overreach. I had an agent tell me she could get me six figures if I left my current agent for her. I told her I didn't think I could earn out an advance that big at that point in my career.

Eventually, I did get a six-figure advance -- in 2007. About two months before the crash. Which means my books didn't have a chance in hell of earning out. That was the first nail in my Berkley coffin.

Remember, it's going to cost your publisher a lot of money to produce that book. If you add a large advance on top of that, you're taking a real gamble. If you don't earn out that advance plus the production costs, you'll lose your contract. More than one author has found herself out in the cold after demanding a six-figure advance she didn't earn out.

If you do write a blockbuster, you'll still get those six figures -- just on the back end when the royalty checks start coming in. That, after all, is what an advance is -- an advance against royalties. I'd rather get it in royalties, though it's going to take longer, than have to worry about screwing up my career.

I've heard agents say that by asking for a lot of money up front, you can force the publisher to spend more in marketing and on a larger print run. (If your print run is too small, you're not going to make the best seller lists no matter what you do. There are simply not enough of your books out there to deliver those kinds of sales.) Personally, I'd rather grow my career before taking a gamble like that.

Editors and Rewrites

As a newbie author, chances are that you don't know the romance market as well as your editor does. If your editor asks for revisions you don't agree with, don't automatically set your heels and refuse. Ask her what the problem is, explain your reservations, and see if the two of you can come up with an alternative you do agree with.

I had that situation with *The Forever Kiss*. When Alex read the first version of the book, she hated it and suggested that I turn Cade McKinnon into a bounty hunter. I didn't feel that would work, and I seriously considered either buying the book back or writing something else for her altogether. Luckily, the editor was able to suggest revisions that addressed the plot elements Alex didn't like. The result was much stronger, and both of us were happy with the way it turned out.

So never refuse to do suggested rewrites. Remember that you and your editor want the same thing: to sell lots of copies of the best book you can write.

Critics, Reviewers, and Fans

One of the facts you need to face is that not everybody is going to love your baby. Never mind that you and your editor think it's marvelous, a certain percentage of people are going to hate it. And they're going to write Amazon reviews and blogs and BookToks telling the whole world your pride and joy sucks.

This is particularly true when you write erotic romance. There are a whole lot of prudes out there who don't want to see romances include anything hotter than a tongue-free kiss. And they will not hesitate to lambaste a book and its author for stepping over the line of what they consider moral decency.

Now, when I was nothing but a *Secrets* author, I didn't see many of those people. I loved reading my Amazon reviews because they were so positive and encouraging. But the minute I became a Berkley author -- and started hitting the best seller list -- the trolls came out in droves.

When I clicked on the other reviews those folks had done, I often found they gave one-star ratings to everything that wasn't a cookbook or a Christian Inspirational romance. Which begs the question: why in the heck were they buying my erotic romance? They had to know they'd find it offensive.

Fact is, I think they were just crusading against what they view as "porn." Bad-mouth a book loudly enough, and you can keep people from buying it.

Of course, sometimes people give you a bad review simply because the book didn't work for them. A bad review can thus give you food for thought by pointing out something you did wrong. So think about the review. Did the writer have a point?

Then again, some people, particularly bloggers,

have built a readership around doing nasty reviews. A woman once wrote a review saying anyone who was lactose intolerant shouldn't read *Jane's Warlord*, because it was so cheesy. She then went on to call Baran a Fabio clone.

Not surprisingly, this really, really ticked me off. When you get reviews like this, particularly in blogs, it's natural to want to fire off a response and pin the reviewer's ears back. *You think it's so easy, you write a book!*

Lie down until that impulse goes away. You gain nothing, zero, zilch from responding to any review. And if you get into a shouting match on X, you can give readers the impression you're a bitch. Like it or not, that reviewer is entitled to express her opinion. Suck it up. Or better yet, don't read her review.

I have learned that there's no better way to give myself writer's block than reading Amazon reviews. The majority of my reviews are very positive, but there's always going to be one or two that would peel the varnish off a bookcase. Do you think I focus on the thirty glowing ones? Heck no. What sticks in my psychic lint trap is the one that says, "I used the pages of this book for toilet paper." So I try not to read Amazon reviews at all.

Then there are the emails. I once got a particularly searing one objecting to the fact that the hero of *Forever Kiss* is a Confederate war veteran. I pointed out that Cade had paid for his slave-owning boyhood by becoming a slave to a vampire sadist for 120 years. Ridgemont tortured him without mercy. (And yes, the irony there was intentional on my part. I wanted Cade to pay for owning slaves and fighting for slavery.)

That was twenty years ago. When Changeling

reissued the book in 2022, I was horrified to realize there were parts of it that were still flat-out radioactive. I rewrote the book to take the offensive crap out.

I should have listened to that reader all those years ago. I think I fixed it, but it was a bitch to do.

In general, however, you're better off simply responding, "Thank you for your opinion. I'll keep that in mind."

That's the downside of the writer gig. The upside is the fans.

I adore my fans. They line up at my table at conventions, stop me in the halls to ask for a picture or my autograph. That last is particularly flattering, because I have the ugliest signature in the free world. There are doctors with more readable handwriting than mine.

Under my fans' tender care, my once scrawny, cringing little ego became as fat and glossy as a large chinchilla. Recent years, however, have put it on a diet again.

No matter how big you get or how much money you make, always treat fans as the treasure they are. Take time to sign their piles of books and smile at them until your cheeks ache. Remember, they buy your books. You owe them.

But you should also keep in mind that some of them may not be fans at all, merely conmen looking to fleece what they imagine is a wealthy romance author. They'll write you asking for free books or money to get a nose job or to buy their imaginary cancer-ridden child a heart transplant.

Don't even respond. Actually, not responding is a good idea when it comes to any email that raises your hackles, particularly if it's from a convict or someone who sounds like a nut.

Nuts want attention. If you give it to them, they can become stalkers. Before long, you'll find yourself hiring a bodyguard to stand outside the ladies' room so you don't get jumped.

Just be careful out there.

If You Don't Have Anything Nice To Say...

Silence is golden, particularly when it comes to the work of other writers you may not like. I don't care if you think she couldn't write her way out of a paper bag, don't you *dare* express that opinion to readers. There's nothing more unprofessional, and there is no better way to shoot yourself in the foot. Word will get back to her, her editor, her publisher, her fans, and her dog, and you will be on everybody's stinky list.

And it should be obvious that you never dis your editor or publisher in public, no matter how ticked off you are. Don't bite the hand that signs your royalty check.

Chapter Twenty: Websites and Promotion

So you've found a publisher. Even now, your book is making its way through the publication process -- which can take anything from two months for an e-pub to a year for a New York print publisher.

Now you've got to make sure readers know it's coming, and that it's worth their time to buy.

In other words, you need to promote your book.

Just how much help can you expect from your publisher? Surprisingly, the bigger a publisher is, the less likely they are to promo your book, particularly if you're a newbie. Changeling Press promotes the hell out of their books, but you're going to need to do your own promotion as well.

It's easy to go broke doing promo, which is why I think newbies should be very selective in what they do. I didn't start doing physical promo at all until my fourth Berkley novel. No bookmarks, no buttons, no nothing. For one thing, I didn't have the money.

If you really must spend money, go to an online printer and make yourself some buttons with your book cover and a clever catch phrase. Readers love them.

Spinning Your Web

Actually, there was one kind of promo I did when I was just starting out: my website. A website is an absolute necessity as an advertising tool, allowing you to reach a large number of readers for very little cash outlay. Even though websites are no longer quite the major force in promo they used to be, I find mine invaluable as a place where I can refer people to check out my backlist.

Newsletters and reader magnets -- free stories

that convince readers to subscribe to the newsletter -- are even better promo. I'd also suggest you make use of TikTok, following other BookTok authors to see what they do to engage readers. X and Facebook also have their place in marketing, since many older readers hang out on FB, and publishing professionals like X.

But don't just post "Buy My Book!" Comment on your hobbies -- Ilona Andrews talks about her knitting -- or discuss the books and films you love. Or your pets. You may not want to post pictures of your kids -- that can get attention you don't want from some horrifying people -- but you can always post pics of your fur baby.

Generating Traffic

The trick with a website is not just to put one up, but to get people to keep coming back. I did this in two ways.

When I was trying to learn how to write back in the early 1990s, I wrote 20 or so erotic romance short stories. When I first set up my website, I rotated those stories on it, and they acted like reader magnets. A lot of people discovered my writing through those stories, and they helped the sales of my *Secrets* work a great deal.

Post free smut, and they will come.

I eventually took the stories off the site when I decided I wanted to go mainstream. I was also worried about kids getting access to the site. Those stories are not suitable teenage reading.

Professional Help

You can also hire a small company that specialize in marketing. I use Coffee Time Romance & More, which has a huge newsletter list. The company does a great job for me.

That said, you should carefully check out any marketing company you're contemplating using. There are predators out there who make their money by preying on newbie authors. Here again is why you'd do well to network with other writers on Facebook and TikTok. If nobody's heard of a particular company, be cautious.

There are many editors available online whom you can hire, including me. However, I'd check out anyone you're considering to make sure they're actually qualified.

Another organization I would recommend is *Passionate Ink*, an online erotic romance writer's group I helped found in the early 2000s. PI was one of the chapters that split off from *Romance Writers of America*. I would strongly suggest joining it. For one thing, it offers a pair of terrific contests for both published and unpublished erotic romance authors. The dues are relatively low, and entirely worth it.

Good Luck!

I'd like to thank you for buying *Passionate Ink: A Guide To Writing Erotic Romance*. If you're just starting out, the road may seem really intimidating, and you may not be sure it's worth pursuing.

All I can tell you is to listen to your heart. For me, there was never any question about whether I'd continue with my fight for publication, no matter how long I had to wait. And it was a long, frustrating fight. As I've said, I decided I wanted to become a writer when I was just nine years old, but I didn't publish my first novel until I was forty-three.

Nor was it from lack of trying. From the time I

was nine, I always had a book going. I wrote and I wrote, and I read everything I could get my hands on, including books like this one. I sent off short story submissions and got insulting rejection letters, but I never quit writing.

I was in college when my father finally asked me why I was doing this to myself when all I ever got was frustration and disappointment. He loves me, and he hates to see me hurt.

I said, "Dad, I write because I can't *not* write." It was a compulsion I couldn't explain, even to him. Writing fed something in me nothing else did, not even art.

Dad was very, very proud when I finally got my first Berkley contract.

If you feel the same restless compulsion to write, keep working. There's a good chance that all that naked drive will pay off in publication. A compulsion like that is usually born of a talent demanding to be used.

But if you just want to write erotic romance because you want to sign autographs and make a ton of money, you're probably wasting your time. You'd have better odds trying to hit the jackpot in Vegas. And it would probably be cheaper.

Write because you love it too much to quit, whether you're ever published or not. If you don't love it like that, you probably shouldn't be a writer.

And only you can answer that question.

Author's Note and Dedication

In 2006, I conducted an online class on writing erotic romance for *Passionate Ink*, then the erotic romance chapter of *Romance Writers of America*. When I finished the class, I had more than a hundred pages of material, which I've expanded into the book you hold in your hands.

I would like to thank the members of *Passionate Ink* for letting me appropriate their chapter name as the title of this book. I'd also like to thank the kind friends who helped make it possible. First, there's my former critique partner, Diane Whiteside, who was always ready to pitch in on whatever project I did. In the case of this book, she culled the best books from her extensive library and penned the bibliography for me.

Next, there's the wonderful SPs of the Angela Knight email loop, who answered a series of questionnaires on their reading tastes. I've quoted their insightful answers throughout the book.

Finally, I'd like to thank you, reader and writer, for picking up this book. I hope you find it helpful as you explore the field of erotic romance.

Appendix 1: Suggested Nonfiction for Romance Writers

There are many good books on writing. I should know; I've been collecting them for years. Here are a few culled from my personal keeper shelves. If you hit Amazon, you'll probably be able to find all kinds of goodies on any given writing problem you have.

Beard, Julie. The Complete Idiot's Guide to Getting Your Romance Published. Alpha Books, January 21, 2000. ISBN: 002863196X.

Bickman, Jack. Scene and Structure (Elements of Fiction Writing). Writer's Digest Books, 1999. ISBN: 0898799066.

Bickman, Jack. The 38 Most Common Fiction Writing Mistakes (And How to Avoid Them.) Writer's Digest Books, 1997. ISBN: 0898798213.

Cowden, Tami D., Caro LaFever and Sue Viders. The Complete Writer's Guide to Heroes and Heroines. Lone Eagle Publishing Co., 2000. ISBN: 1580650244. *(This is one you really need. It's a huge help.)*

Dixon, Debra. Goal, Motivation & Conflict: The Building Blocks of Good Fiction. Gryphon Books for Writers, 1996. ISBN: 0965437108. *(Get this, if you don't get anything else.)*

Levin, Donna. Get that Novel Written.

Writer's Digest Books, 2001. ISBN: 1582971358.

McKee, Robert. <u>Story: Substance, Structure, Style and the Principles of Screenwriting</u>. ReganBooks, 1997. ISBN: 0060391685. *(This may technically be a book on screenwriting, but you'll find it very useful in writing any kind of fiction.)*

Tobias, Ronald. <u>20 Master Plots (And How to Build Them)</u>. Writer's Digest Books, 2003. ISBN:1582972397.

Truss, Lynne. <u>Eats, Shoots and Leaves: The Zero Tolerance Approach to Punctuation</u>. Gotham, 2004. ISBN: 1592400876.

Appendix 2: Bibliography

Many thanks to my friend and critique partner, Diane Whiteside, who compiled the following bibliographies of recommended reading for the erotic romance author.

Diane Whiteside's Erotic Bibliography

The Starter Bookshelf, Part 1

Erotic Encyclopedias

If you own nothing else, own these books. In my opinion, these two books are complementary. However, some people, because of their topical overlap, prefer one or the other:

> Joannides, Paul. <u>Guide to Getting It On</u>! Ebury Press, 2004. ISBN: 0091856981. *(This book covers almost everything in a very approachable, nonjudgmental fashion. There are multiple editions, all of which are excellent. It's written by a guy, which doesn't get in the way. But occasionally I find his slightly different perspective to be very useful.)*

> Winks, Cathy and Anne Semans. <u>The Good Vibrations Guide to Sex: The Most Complete Sex Manual Ever Written</u>. Cleis Press, 2005. ISBN: 157344158. *(If it's not the most complete sex manual ever written, it surely tried to be that. It's written by two very experienced sex educators and is a useful counterweight to Paul Joannides' book. The topics discussed overlap but the material isn't*

identical.)

Commonly Discussed Topics

Blue, Violet. <u>The Ultimate Guide to Cunnilingus: How to Go Down on a Woman and Give Her Exquisite Pleasure</u>. Cleis Press, 2002. ISBN: 1573441449. *(Written by a top sex educator, it tells about all of the aspects in great detail. It also includes short stories by erotica author Alison Tyler, illustrating each topic's emotional impact.)*

Blue, Violet. <u>The Ultimate Guide to Fellatio: How to Go Down on a Man and Give Him Mind-Blowing Pleasure</u>. Cleis Press, 2002. ISBN: 1573441511. *(Written by a top sex educator, it tells about all of the aspects in great detail. It also includes short stories by erotica author Alison Tyler, illustrating each topic's emotional impact.)*

Hooper, Anne. <u>Anne Hooper's Kama Sutra: Classic Lovemaking Techniques Reinterpreted for Today's Lovers</u>. Dorling Kindersley Limited, 1994. ISBN: 1564586499. *(This is my personal favorite of the books describing and picturing positions and techniques from the great oriental picture books: the Kama Sutra, Ananga Ranga, and Perfumed Garden. It explains the fitness levels required, the breathing techniques utilized, and the resulting sensations. But everyone has their own preferences for favorite book of this type.)*

Hooper, Anne. <u>Kama Sutra for 21st Century</u>

Lovers. DK Adult, 2003. ISBN: 0789496550. *(This is the in-print version of this book.)*

Morin, Jack. Anal Pleasure and Health. Down There Press, 1998. ISBN: 0960232494. *(Please read this book before writing an anal sex scene. It gives the scientific background and it's accurate enough to be regularly used by medical practitioners.)*

Rogers, Ben R. & Joel Perry. Going Down: The Essential Guide to Oral Sex. Alyson Publications, 2002. ISBN: 1555837522. *(Much as I appreciate Violet Blue's thorough coverage of the subject, the fact remains that she's a girl and she's serious. Rogers & Perry's book is very funny -- and very male-centered. A must-read if you want to write a love scene from the male point-of-view.)*

Contemporary Attitudes

Em & Lo. Nerve's Guide to Sex Etiquette for Ladies and Gentlemen. Plume, 2004. ISBN: 0452285097. *(Very, very funny -- and all too believable.)*

The Writers at Nerve. The Big Bang: A Guide to the New Sexual Universe. Plume, 2003. ISBN: 0452284260. *(This encyclopedic guide by Nerve.com's columnists Em and Lo is sassy, hilarious and fully illustrated. It's both accurate and a look inside current attitudes for those from a slightly different generation.)*

Extra Credit

Hartley, Nina. <u>Nina's Guide to Oral Sex</u>. (DVD) Includes <u>Nina's Guide to Fellatio</u> and <u>Nina's Guide to Cunnilingus</u>. *(Nina Hartley's How-To guides are accurate and work hard to show what really happens when someone's enjoying themselves, rather than what makes the best camera angle for a porn movie. The examples are heterosexual and bisexual.)*

Lou Paget's great trio of how-to books, based on her clinics. Her combination of humor and frankness is incredibly appealing and relaxing to me. Others may be more comprehensive but she's incredibly good at putting me in the mood to write a love scene:

<u>The Big O: How to Have Them, Give Them, and Keep Them Coming</u>. Judy Piatkus Publishers Ltd (January 24, 2002). ISBN: 0749922923.

<u>How to Give Her Absolute Pleasure: Totally Explicit Techniques Every Woman Wants Her Man to Know</u>. Broadway, 2000. ISBN: 0767904524.

<u>How to Be a Great Lover: Girlfriend-to-Girlfriend Totally Explicit Techniques that Will Blow His Mind</u>. Broadway, 1999. ISBN: 0767902874.

Diane Whiteside's Erotic Bibliography

The Starter Bookshelf, Part 2 -- Angela Knight asked me for my favorite reference books for writing BDSM-flavored scenes. This list is slanted toward female authors writing heterosexual scenes.

Hope it helps you too --

Diane Whiteside

Introductory Books

There is no such thing as an encyclopedia of BDSM. However, there are good introductory books that cover a large number of topics in encouraging, nonjudgmental tones. In my opinion, these two books are complementary. However, some people, because of their topical overlap, prefer one or the other:

Miller, Philip and Molly Devon. Screw the Roses, Send Me the Thorns: The Romance and Sexual Sorcery of Sadomasochism. Mystic Rose Books, 1988. ISBN: 0964596008. *(This book covers almost everything in a very chatty, friendly fashion with lots of illustrations and details. It's definitely heterosexually focused, with a male dominant and a female submissive.)*

Wiseman, Jay. SM 101: A Realistic Introduction. Greenery Press, 1998. ISBN: 0963976389. *(This is an honest introduction, written by a man who's been in the scene for over 25 years and is a retired paramedic. It includes perspectives from bisexuals, lesbians, female dominants, etc., which are lacking in Miller and Devon's book.)*

Must haves

One commentator remarked that a BDSM is like chocolate ice cream: 98 percent vanilla ice cream and 2 percent chocolate. But all you remember is the chocolate. As a writer, if you already understand how to write a vanilla erotic scene, in order to turn it into a BDSM, all you have to know is how to add the 2 percent BDSM twist. But I have found very few books that clearly explain how to do this from a heterosexual perspective:

> Warren, John, Ph.D. <u>The Loving Dominant</u>. Revised, updated second edition. Greenery Press, 2000. ISBN: 1890159204. *(This is actually an excellent introduction to BDSM that includes information for dominants of all genders and orientations. But John is an Alpha male with a protective streak a mile wide. He explains very clearly why he does things and why they have such a strong effect on his submissive. Once you have read and absorbed this book, you'll be prepared to create almost any BDSM scene imaginable.)*

Commonly Discussed Topics

> Campbell, Drew. <u>The Bride Wore Black Leather... and he looked fabulous!: An Etiquette Guide for the Rest of Us</u>. Greenery Press, 2002. ISBN: 1573441449. *(When you're writing about situations that aren't covered by the usual dictates of common sense, this is a starting point. It's wonderfully matter-of-fact and superbly illustrated, too.)*

Easton, Dossie & Janet W. Hardy. The New Bottoming Book. Greenery Press, 2001. ISBN: 1890159352. *(This book teaches that "bottoming" (or being a "submissive," or a "masochist") is just as much an art and worthy of respect as being a "top" (or a "dominant" or a "sadist"). It also delves into the why and how, with some wonderfully insightful anecdotes.)*

Easton, Dossie & Janet W. Hardy. The New Topping Book. Greenery Press, 2003. ISBN: 1890159360. *(This book is a legendary starting point for tops, especially in its discussion of ethics and rituals.)*

Moser, Charles, Ph.D., M.D. and J.J. Madeson. Bound to be Free: The SM Experience. The Continuum Publ. Co., 1996. ISBN: 0826410472. *(Cowritten by an SM practitioner and a therapist specializing in SM behavior, this book was the first to explore sadomasochism from both a clinical and practicing point of view. I find this book the most useful of the academic studies because it's written in the most approachable language.)*

Wiseman, Jay. Jay Wiseman's Erotic Bondage Handbook. Greenery Press, 2000. ISBN: 18900159131. *(This is the must-have book for bondage, no matter what technique you intend to use or how experienced you are in tying knots. It includes a full discussion of how to prepare the scene, the equipment, and the risks involved.)*

Brame, William and Gloria Brame. Different Loving: The World of Sexual Dominance and Submission. Villard, 1996. ISBN: 0679769560. (*Written in very dry language, this is a very solid overview of BDSM. If you're researching the more unusual BDSM practices (e.g., golden showers, infantilism), read this and/or Moser and Madeson books before you hit the websites.*)

Midori. The Seductive Art of Japanese Bondage. Greenery Press, 2001. ISBN: 1890159387. (*Japanese rope bondage is legendary for being both beautiful and difficult. Midori's book shows very clearly how to do it and includes some beautiful illustrations, which bring rope bondage's attraction to life.*)

Original Synopsis Of *Master Of The Moon*
Here I've included the original synopsis of *Master of the Moon*. Note that it's written in present tense, as is traditional for synopses. You should also reveal how you resolve all the conflicts.

Synopsis: Mistress Of The Moon
by Angela Knight

Diana London is the city manager for Verdaville, a struggling South Carolina textile town with a population of five thousand. At thirty-two, Diana's biological clock is ticking down on her ambition to become a mother, but her age isn't her biggest problem in starting a family.

Her biggest problem is that she's a werewolf.

Diana is a member of a race of werewolves created by Merlin sixteen hundred years ago. His intention was that if the magic using Majae and Magi he'd created ever turned on humanity, his Direkind werewolves would destroy the traitors. So unlike the Magekind, with their elaborate network operating behind the scenes of human history, the Direkind remain isolated, hidden and secret.

Diana's Direkind parents raised her and her brother James to be as thoroughly middle class as their werewolf nature allows. But now Diana is in the midst of her yearly Burning Moon -- the month when, in other words, she's in heat. Men instinctively respond to the pheromones in Diana's scent, but she doesn't dare let one of them seduce her.

During her Burning Moon, her saliva carries the agents to transform her partner into a werewolf, and not every man can be trusted with that power. She can't risk so much as a kiss without being absolutely sure of her partner. So despite her need, Diana knows she must keep her distance from men.

At least until she meets *Llyr Galatyn*, king of the Cachamwri Sidhe. A magical being himself, the fairy king is immune to her kiss, and thus a safe partner.

But Llyr carries heavy baggage of his own. His brother, *Ansgar Galatyn*, has been trying to have him assassinated for sixteen centuries so Ansgar can rule their two kingdoms.

Normally, Llyr would call his brother out and be done with it, but under the terms of his father's will, the first brother who lifts his hand against the other will lose all claim to either throne. And there are enough of the old man's supporters in both kingdoms to make sure his directives stick.

Yet Ansgar realized that the wording of the will was such that if someone else killed Llyr, Ansgar could succeed to both thrones. All he has to do was make sure the murder couldn't be traced back to him.

So over the centuries, Ansgar's hired killers have slain Llyr's four wives and ten children in the course of these murder attempts. Llyr has never been able to prove that his brother was behind the murders. He's considered hiring assassins of his own to eliminate Ansgar, but his sense of honor won't allow him to play the same games with his father's will.

Instead, he struggles with a heavy burden of guilt for the deaths of his family. He also feels driven to do whatever is necessary to keep his people from falling under Ansgar's ruthless dominion.

To add to his burden, Llyr has recently lost yet another woman he'd loved: Janieda, who gave her life for his in the previous book, Master of the Night. Her death on top of the others' has convinced him that any woman he loves is doomed.

The story begins when Diana and Llyr share an erotic dream, though they have never met. Llyr realizes he's destined to meet his dream lover. The idea inspires a certain nagging guilt, but he's still male enough to be a little intrigued.

The next day, Diana too, struggles with the effects of her Burning Moon and her memories of the dream. Her problems increase when she's called to the scene of a horrific murder. The male victim was found nude, gutted and spreadeagled in his own bed, with his throat ripped out and his genitals mutilated.

Having learned Diana's secret the year before, Police Chief BILL GIST asks her to use her powers to learn what she can about the killer. Assuming the guise of a wolf, Diana tracks the murderer's scent into the woods.

There she confronts *Susan Carter*, a murderous magic-using vampire created by Geirolf, the demonic villain who died in Master of the Night. After a short struggle, Carter uses her powers to escape her shape-changing enemy, leaving Diana to worry who'll be the vampire's next victim.

Meanwhile, Llyr fends off an assassination attempt from four of his own bodyguards before meeting with his new Magekind allies. He's agreed to help Arthur recapture Geirolf's escaped vampire offspring in exchange for the Magekind's help in dealing with his brother.

Llyr is surprised when his allies show him a copy of a newspaper which shows his dream lover at the scene of one of the murders. He agrees to investigate the slaying to determine if it is indeed one of the escaped vampires, knowing this is his chance to meet Diana.

When Diana talks to Gist the next day, she's surprised to learn the FBI has taken over the case. Diana questions the chief about this, since murder is a state crime and the bureau has no jurisdiction. The chief's dazed responses convince her he's actually under some sort of spell. And that means the so-called FBI agents are nothing of the kind.

Storming downstairs to confront the chief's magical attackers, Diana finds his office occupied by Llyr and three of his bodyguards, all dressed up as the agents they're pretending to be.

She and the bodyguards almost come to blows, but Llyr introduces himself. Diana recognizes him as the man from her dream, and the erotic tension begins to steam between them.

Llyr tells Diana they need to work together to solve the murder, explaining the circumstances. She's scornful at first, so he transports them all to his palace. There, surrounded by magic and universe full of enchanted creatures, Diana has no choice but to accept his word. Though she's reluctant to admit it, she finds his powers intimidating.

Meanwhile, Llyr backs off his assumption that his dream means they're destined to fall in love. She doesn't seem his usual type. Still, those pheromones she gives off are very tempting, and he toys with the idea of a little no-strings sex with the luscious werewolf.

As Llyr and Diana circle each other, a spy among Llyr's court decides that she needs to report these events to Ansgar. She transports herself to the enemy king's palace and tells him what she's seen. Ansgar is intrigued, and even more fascinated by the news that Llyr plans to work with this werewolf female. He decides to keep an eye on the proceedings.

Llyr begins his campaign to seduce Diana, who decides he'll make a safe partner. After all, since he's a magical being, she can't infect him. Besides, he's driving her out of her mind.

But when the two make wild love, each gets more than he bargained for. Llyr's powers and seductive skill intrigue Diana, while her uninhibited animal passion make her the hottest lover he's ever had.

Afterwards, Diana, Llyr and the bodyguards return to Earth. But even as she helps them check into a hotel, Susan is seducing her next victim.

Meanwhile, Diana gets a call from her brother, Jim London, who will be the hero of the next book. Bemused, Diana tells him about her experiences in the Mageverse, then has to talk fast to keep her protective little brother from coming to Verdaville and kicking fairy ass.

No sooner does she hang up than she gets yet another call. This one however, is from Gist, who tells her there's been another murder. She contacts Llyr and tells him to meet her at the crime scene.

They find that Susan has viciously murdered yet another man. But as they start investigating, they're interrupted by a group of reporters demanding to know what happened. Llyr uses his abilities to magically influence the entire bunch into leaving.

Meanwhile, Ansgar, in disguise, watches the proceedings from the crowd, noting the obvious sparks between Diana and Llyr with sinister interest.

After the run in with the reporters, Diana and Llyr argue about his high-handed use of his powers. She doesn't like to see even reporters misused, and besides, too much splashy magic could raise questions she really doesn't want to answer.

Llyr, being Llyr, turns the argument into another sizzling seduction.

When she staggers home afterward, Diana finds herself questioning what she's doing getting involved with this arrogantly seductive fairy king. True, he makes the Burning Moon more bearable, but he's also a very dangerous man, not to mention a pain in the butt.

Meanwhile, Llyr's bodyguards indignantly approach Llyr about Diana, whom they believe is far too uppity for a mortal. When Llyr finds himself jumping to her defense, he begins to wonder whether he's getting too attached to a woman who really isn't his type.

While all this is going on, Ansgar tracks down Susan in her lair. The two get into a vicious brawl. Susan, flush with power, gives the Sidhe king more of a fight than he expected, but he still wins.

Instead of killing her, Ansgar reveals the whole confrontation was a test. He tells her he's impressed by her creative viciousness, and he offers her a deal: he'll give her even more power if she'll take care of his inconvenient brother. She agrees, only to scream and beg for mercy as Ansgar begins pumping a burning flood of magical power into her.

The next night, Llyr, intent on proving that Diana is nothing but a sexual toy, dominates her in a sizzling encounter she finds both arousing and infuriating. She storms off to lick her wounds.

Susan has kept them under surveillance while recovering from the process of gaining her new power. She decides this is the perfect opportunity to strike.

The vampire attacks Llyr and his bodyguards at the motel with her borrowed power in a magical assault that blows away half the wing of the motel.

In the battle royale that follows, the bodyguards

are killed, and Susan's spell strips Llyr of his magic. But even powerless, Llyr isn't a foe to take lightly. He manages to injure her before making his own escape. Wounded, powerless, and furious, he staggers into the woods.

Diana is at home brooding her way through a gallon of chocolate ice cream when she hears on her police scanner that a huge explosion has just destroyed a wing of the motel -- the same wing that houses Llyr and his men.

She arrives at the scene to discover the bodyguard's corpses, but no Llyr. Frantic, she transforms into a wolf and follows Llyr's scent trail into the nearby woods. There she finds him badly hurt, but alive.

Diana takes Llyr home with her and treats his injuries herself, since, as a non-human, he doesn't dare go to a hospital.

Being powerless and ill for the first time in his life is agonizing for Llyr. He also finds himself shamed, because Diana, whom he'd sexually humiliated, is uncharacteristically patient and far more nurturing than he would have suspected.

Llyr apologies to her for his treatment of her, which surprises her. She'd thought he was too rigid and conscious of his own royalty to bend that much.

Meanwhile, Ansgar and Susan meet. He's furious that the assassination failed, and warns her that the next one had better succeed.

Since Llyr has no way to contact his own people without his powers, Diana appoints herself his bodyguard, which irks him. But knowing that without her help, he could end up dead, he forces himself to graciously accept.

Trying to atone for being a bastard earlier, he

makes sweet, tender love to her. Diana begins to wonder if she's falling for him, an idea she finds truly frightening. She knows he'll eventually regain his powers and return to the Mageverse.

Susan needs to feed to restore her strength after healing her injuries from her fight with Llyr and his guard. She decides to seduce Gist. The chief, however, is not interested, so Susan simply abducts him.

Diana and Llyr take part in the resulting manhunt to find the kidnapped cop. They managed to find the two before Susan can kill him. The vampire, her powers drained, is unwilling to tangle with them again and takes to her heels. She decides she's going to have to get rid of Diana if she's going to have a chance at Llyr.

Susan asks Ansgar to kill Diana for her, reasoning that with the werewolf gone, Llyr will be much easier to kill.

The two spring their trap. Susan lures Diana away from Llyr, and Ansgar launches his magical attack on her. Meanwhile Susan doubles back to attack Llyr, taunting him that Ansgar is going to butcher his lover.

Ansgar transports Diana to the Mageverse, where he gloats over his plans to kill her in some way that will torment and humiliate his hated brother. Truly helpless for the first time in her life, she can only rage at him in werewolf form.

Meanwhile, Llyr manages to kill Susan in their battle, despite his lack of magic.

Desperate to save Diana, Llyr breaks through the barrier keeping him from his power and goes after the two on the Mageverse.

Ansgar is astonished and frightened when he appears, bloodied and bloodthirsty with rage. He reminds Llyr that under the terms of his father's will, if either of them lifts a hand against the other, he will lose all right to the throne.

This stops Llyr for a moment as he sees the trap he's in. Ansgar begins to gloat, preparing to kill yet another of his hated brother's loved ones.

Llyr attacks him anyway, reasoning that he'd rather give up his crown than let Ansgar kill Diana. In the battle that follows, Diana manages to free herself and help him kill Ansgar.

But before they can enjoy their victory, they're confronted by Ansgar's guard and the rest of his subjects. There's no way Diana and Llyr can fight them all off. Instead, Diana makes a passionate argument that a leader must be worthy of his crown.

Ansgar has been violating the spirit of his father's directive for centuries, yet Llyr never once sent his own assassins. Which of the two is truly more fit to rule?

The leader of Ansgar's nobles, eager to step into his place, orders their deaths anyway. As Diana and Llyr prepare to fight a battle they know they'll lose, they're astonished when members of Ansgar's guard and court defect to join them.

It turns out they all remember the old king and his youngest son fondly, and they have no desire to be ruled by any of Ansgar's sycophants.

Diana watches Llyr as he establishes control over his unified kingdom. She realizes again how thoroughly out of her league she is. Llyr's grateful grandmother, seeing her unhappiness, offers her anything she wants. She asks to be sent back home.

Llyr quickly realizes Diana has vanished. Flushed with victory and eager to share his triumph, he goes to her. When she tells him how far out of her league he is, he tells her how thoroughly she's proven otherwise. He begs her to be his queen.

She finally agrees, and the two make love, knowing they'll soon have a royal wedding to plan.

Angela Knight

New York Times best-selling author Angela Knight has written and published more than sixty novels, novellas, and ebooks, including the Mageverse and Merlin's Legacy series. With a career spanning more than two decades, *Romantic Times Bookclub Magazine* has awarded her their Career Achievement award in Paranormal Romance, as well as two Reviewers' Choice awards for Best Erotic Romance and Best Werewolf Romance.

Angela is currently a writer, editor, and cover artist for Changeling Press LLC. She also teaches online writing courses. Besides her fiction work, Angela's writing career includes a decade as an award-winning South Carolina newspaper reporter. She lives in South Carolina with her husband, Michael, a thirty-plus year police veteran and detective with a local police department.

Angela at Changeling: changelingpress.com /angela-knight-a-26

Made in United States
Orlando, FL
15 July 2024

49011477R00147